GED® TEST
Science Prep 2015

KAPLAN

PUBLISHING

New York

ACKNOWLEDGEMENTS

Special thanks to the team that made this book possible:
Arthur Ahn, Mikhail Alexeeff, Gina Allison, Kim Bowers, Erik Bowman, Julie Choi, Margaret Crane, Alisha Crowley, Lola Dart, Boris Dvorkin, Paula Fleming, Tom Flesher, Joanna Graham, Allison Harm, Gar Hong, Kevin Jacobson, Wyatt Kent, Jennifer Land, Heather Maigur, Terrence McGovern, Eli Meyer, Kathy Osmus, Anthony Parr, Rachel Pearsall, Neha Rao, Rachel Reina, Teresa Rupp, Scott Safir, Glen Stohr, Alexandra Strelka, Lee Weiss, and many others who have shaped this book over the years.

GED® is a registered trademark of the American Council on Education (ACE) and may not be used without permission. The GED® and GED Testing Service® brands are administered by GED Testing Service LLC under license. ACE and GED Testing Service LLC have not approved, authorized, endorsed, been involved in the development of, or licensed the substantive content of this material.

This publication is designed to provide accurate information in regard to the subject matter covered as of its publication date, with the understanding that knowledge and best practice constantly evolve. The publisher is not engaged in rendering medical, legal, accounting, or other professional service. If medical or legal advice or other expert assistance is required, the services of a competent professional should be sought. This publication is not intended for use in clinical practice or the delivery of medical care. To the fullest extent of the law, neither the Publisher nor the Editors assume any liability for any injury and/or damage to persons or property arising out of or related to any use of the material contained in this book.

Published by Kaplan Publishing, a division of Kaplan, Inc.
395 Hudson Street
New York, NY 10014

Printed in the United States of America

10 9 8 7 6 5 4 3 2 1

ISBN: 978-1-62523-238-0

Kaplan Publishing books are available at special quantity discounts to use for sales promotions, employee premiums, or educational purposes. For more information or to purchase books, please call the Simon & Schuster special sales department at 866-506-1949.

CONTENTS

KAPLAN'S GED® SCIENCE TEST BOOK AND ONLINE CENTER

Congratulations on your decision to pursue high school equivalency, and thank you for choosing Kaplan for your GED® test preparation.

You've made the right choice in acquiring this book—you're now armed with a GED® Science test preparation program that is the result of years of researching the GED® tests and teaching thousands of students the skills they need to succeed. You have what you need to pass the GED® Science test and score higher; the next step is to make the commitment to your study plan.

The next section will tell you everything you need to know to take advantage of your book and your Online Center.

YOUR BOOK

This book contains a complete study program, including the following:

- Detailed instruction covering the essential concepts for Science
- Time-tested and effective methods and strategies for every question type
- A Pretest designed to help you diagnose your strengths and weaknesses
- Hundreds of practice questions, followed by answer explanations
- A timed, full-length Science Practice Test

YOUR ONLINE CENTER

Your Kaplan Online Center gives you access to additional instruction and practice materials to reinforce key concepts and sharpen your GED® test skills. The following list summarizes the resources available to you:

- An additional full-length Science Practice Test, so that you can practice the computer-based question formats used on the actual test
- Analysis of your performance on your Practice Test, including detailed answer explanations for the computer-based practice test
- Video lessons featuring Kaplan's top instructors

GETTING STARTED

Studying for the GED® test can be daunting, and with so many resources available to you, it may not be clear where to begin. Don't worry; we'll break it down one step at a time, just as we will with the GED® test questions that you will soon be on your way to mastering.

GETTING STARTED

1. Take the diagnostic Pretest.
2. Create a study plan.
3. Register your Online Center.
4. Learn and practice using both this book and your Online Center.
5. Work through the Practice Tests to gauge your progress.

STEP 1: TAKE THE DIAGNOSTIC PRETEST

It's essential to take the diagnostic Pretest before you begin to study. Doing so will give you the initial feedback and diagnostic information that you will need to achieve your maximum score. Place enough importance on completing the Pretest—turn off your cell phone, give the tests your full attention, and learn from your performance.

Once you have finished your Pretest, check your answers starting on page 16. Mark the questions that you got correct and **carefully read the answer explanations** of those that you got wrong.

When you have finished the Pretest, make a list of the questions that you got correct and use that list to fill out the Kaplan GED® Test Study Planner on page 20. Use the results to target your weak areas.

Another option is for you to go online and enter your answers so that the Kaplan Online Center can generate your results. Note which sections and which question types you need to target.

Review the detailed answer explanations in the book to better understand your performance. Look for patterns in the questions you answered correctly and incorrectly. Were you stronger in some areas than in others? This analysis will help you target your study time to specific concepts.

STEP 2: CREATE A STUDY PLAN

Use what you've learned from your initial Pretest to identify areas for closer study and practice. Take time to familiarize yourself with the key components of your book and Online Center. Think about how many hours you can consistently devote to GED® test study.

Schedule time for study, practice, and review. It works best for many people to block out short, frequent periods of study time throughout the week. Check in with yourself frequently to make sure you're not falling behind your plan or forgetting about any of your resources.

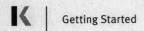

STEP 3: REGISTER YOUR ONLINE CENTER

Register your Online Center using these simple steps:

1. Go to **kaptest.com/booksonline**.
2. Follow the on-screen instructions for GED®. Please have your book available.

Access to the Online Center is limited to the original owner of this book and is nontransferable. Kaplan is not responsible for providing access to the Online Center to customers who purchase or borrow used copies of this book. Access to the Online Center expires one year after you register.

STEP 4: LEARN AND PRACTICE

Your book and Online Center come with many opportunities to develop and practice the skills you'll need on Test Day. Depending on how much time you have to study, you can do this work methodically, covering every unit and lesson, or you can focus your study on those content areas that are most challenging to you. You will inevitably need more work in some areas than in others, but the more thoroughly you prepare, the better your score will be.

Initially, your practice should focus on mastering the needed skills and not on timing. Add timing to your practice as you become familiar with skills and methods.

STEP 5: WORK THROUGH THE PRACTICE TESTS

As you move through your GED® studies, take advantage both the full-length Science Practice Test available in this book and also the one in your Online Center.

Review your Practice Test results thoroughly to make sure you are addressing the areas that are most important to your score. Allot time to review the detailed explanations so that you can learn from your mistakes and review the relevant chapters in the book for additional study.

If you find that you would like access to more of Kaplan's instructional content or practice material, look into our other subject books, our comprehensive GED® preparation books, or our On Demand course option available at **kaptest.com/GED**.

Thanks for choosing Kaplan. We wish you the best of luck on your journey to completing your high school equivalency and taking a vital step toward college and career readiness.

GED® TEST OVERVIEW

The GED® test is a widely used examination that demonstrates high school equivalency as well as college and career readiness. It includes the reading, writing, thinking, and problem-solving skills needed for postsecondary educational programs and for the world of work. This means that your high school equivalency diploma is not an end in itself—it is the springboard to more education, to better-paying jobs, and to more rewarding career paths.

TAKE FOUR SUBTESTS IN FOUR CONTENT AREAS

Reasoning through Language Arts—2.5 hours (one 10-minute break)

- Roughly 50–55 questions
- Includes 1 extended written response to reading passages—up to 45 minutes

Mathematical Reasoning—1 hour, 55 minutes

- Roughly 40–45 questions
- First section—5 questions, no calculator allowed
- Second section—calculator allowed (Texas Instruments TI-30XS MultiView™ calculator)

Social Studies—1.5 hours

- Roughly 30–35 questions
- Includes 1 extended written response to passages and/or graphics—up to 25 minutes

Science—1.5 hours

- Roughly 30–35 questions
- Includes 2 short-answer written responses to passages and/or graphics—up to 10 minutes each

You can read detailed information about the test in the *About the Test* section.

RESPOND TO SEVEN COMPUTER-BASED QUESTION FORMATS

To test a range of skills, the GED® test uses a variety of computer-based question formats. You will see examples of each type of question in *GED® Computer-Based Testing* and in the *About the Test* section. When you take the test, you will use these question formats:

- **Multiple-choice**—click to choose from four choices (A through D).
- **Fill-in-the-blank**—type a word, a phrase, or numbers in a box.
- **Drag-and-drop**—move words, numbers, or objects across the computer screen.
- **Drop-down**—select from menus embedded in text on the computer screen.
- **Hot spot**—click on graphics on the computer.
- **Short-answer**—write a paragraph or two of explanation in response to passages or graphics or a combination of the two.
- **Extended response**—compose a well-developed and supported response to passages or graphics or a combination of the two.

READ AND WRITE THROUGHOUT THE TEST

You will read and interpret passages and word problems on all four tests. In addition, three out of four subtests (*Reasoning through Language Arts, Social Studies,* and *Science*) require that you read a passage or two and compose a response about what you have read.

The type of writing that you will use is called *evidence-based writing*, which means that you need to cite specific evidence from the readings in your response. This is a key characteristic of the type of writing that is required in workplaces and in educational programs. This book contains special lessons and practice activities to help you write effectively on all three of the subtests.

PERFORM MATH SKILLS THROUGHOUT THE TEST

In addition to the questions on the *Mathematical Reasoning Test*, math items also appear on the *Science Test* and the *Social Studies Test*.

On all three of these tests, you may use either a hand-held or an on-screen version of the Texas Instruments TI-30XS MultiView™ calculator to use with math items. If you wish to use a hand-held version of the calculator, you may need to take one with you on test day. **You are strongly encouraged to purchase a hand-held version of this calculator to use with this study guide**. You can buy this calculator at stores that carry office and school supplies and through online vendors. See the section entitled *How to Use the Calculator* for instruction about calculator functions.

USE THE GED TESTING SERVICE® MYGED™ INTERNET PORTAL

MyGED™ is a personalized online program that will be your entry point to all test activities, including scheduling testing and retesting (if necessary), viewing score reports, ordering transcripts and your diploma, and investigating your next steps in making the transition to college or to a career.

TAKE THE TEST: UNDERSTAND YOUR SCORE

Each GED® Test is scored on a scale from 100 to 200. There are three possible scores that you can receive on the GED® Test:

- **Not Passing**—lower than 150 on any of the four tests. You can reschedule up to two times a year to retake any or all of the tests.
- **GED® Passing Score**—at or higher than the minimum score (150 per test) needed to demonstrate high school equivalency–level skills and knowledge. Points on one test do not carry over to the others; that is, if you score 200 on one and 100 on another, that is not equivalent to scoring 150 on both. You need to score 150 on each of the four tests.
- **GED® Score with Honors**—at or higher than the minimum needed (170 per test) to demonstrate career and college readiness

Your score is determined by the number of points you earn on each test, but questions vary in point value. Therefore, there is no fixed number of questions you need to get correct on each test in order to pass or pass with honors.

GED® COMPUTER-BASED TESTING

The GED® Test is delivered on a computer. That means that you will need to familiarize yourself with basic computer skills and computer-based question formats in order to succeed on the test.

NOTE: *The GED® Test on computer is only offered at official Pearson Vue Testing Centers. Any Internet-based test that claims to be the GED® Test is <u>not</u> the actual test. At the MyGED™ portal, you can access study resources, take a practice test, or schedule your test. You cannot take the real GED® test online.*

To become familiar with the computer-based functions, you should review the GED® Test Tutorial available through the GED® Testing Services website. Before you take the actual test, you can practice computer-based testing functions with the Practice Test available in Kaplan's Online Center and with the GED® Testing Service's GED Ready™ Test.

COMPUTER-BASED TESTING FUNCTIONS AND TOOLS

The GED® Test uses many computer **functions**, some of which you may already know. It also offers specific **tools** that you will utilize in different test areas.

 Use the **mouse** to

Tab through the pages of a reading passage

> ⚠ Flag for Review
>
> page 1 | page 2 | page 3 | page 4 | page 5
>
> Excerpt from: *The Story of My Life*
>
> 1   Mr. West from Peoria, Ill. had another man, his wife, a son Clay about 20 years of age and his daughter, America, eighteen. Unfortunately Mr. West had gone to the extreme of providing himself with such a heavy wagon and load that they were deemed objectionable as fellow argonauts. After disposing of some of their supplies they were allowed to join us. They had four fine oxen. This wagon often got stalled in bad roads much to the annoyance of all, but as he was a wagon maker and his companion a blacksmith by trade and both were accommodating there were always ready hands to "pry the wheel out of mire."
>
> 2   A mule team from Washington, D.C. was very insufficiently provisioned . . . [by] a Southern gentlemen "unused to work. . . ." They deserted the train at Salt Lake as they could not proceed with their equipment and it was easier to embrace Mormonism than to brave the "American Desert."
>
> 3   Much in contrast to these men were four batchelors Messers Wilson, Goodall, Fifield and Martin, who had a wagon drawn by four oxen and two milch cows following behind. The latter gave milk all the way to the sink of the Humboldt where they died, having acted as draught animals
>
> What did Mr. West do that allowed his group to join the wagon train?
>
> ○ A.   make wagons for the others
>
> ○ B.   bring four fine oxen
>
> ○ C.   offer milk to the children
>
> ○ D.   leave some of his possessions behind
>
> ← Previous | Next →

Scroll up and down a page when a scroll bar appears

Click on Previous and Next navigation buttons to move forward or backward

Use the **mouse** to (continued)

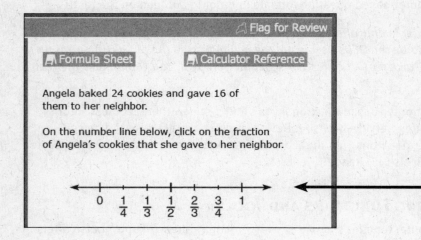

Click on an answer choice, a "Select" menu, or a point on a graphic

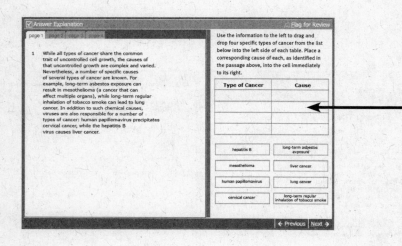

Drag and drop text, numbers, or images into a shape on the computer screen

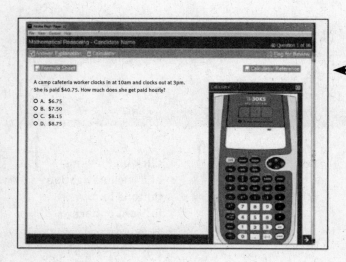

Click to open, move, and close information windows and math resources—such as the calculator, formula sheet, or symbol toolbar

Use **word processing skills** to

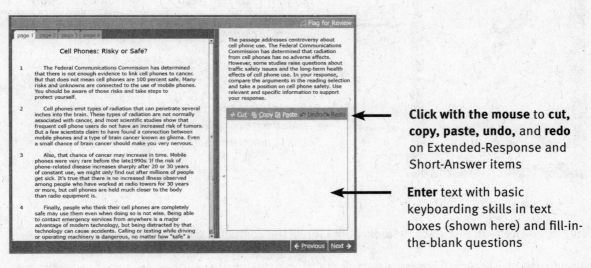

Click with the mouse to **cut, copy, paste, undo,** and **redo** on Extended-Response and Short-Answer items

Enter text with basic keyboarding skills in text boxes (shown here) and fill-in-the-blank questions

Use **the online highlighter,** operated with your mouse, to

Highlight specific information that you will use as evidence in writing your Extended Responses and Short Answers.

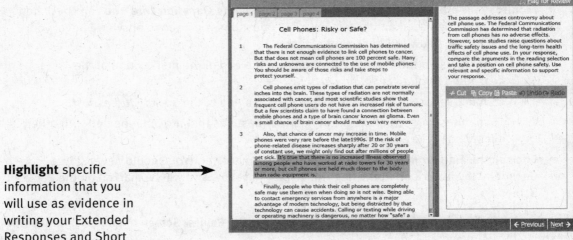

Use the offline, **erasable wipe-off board**, which will be provided at the testing center, to

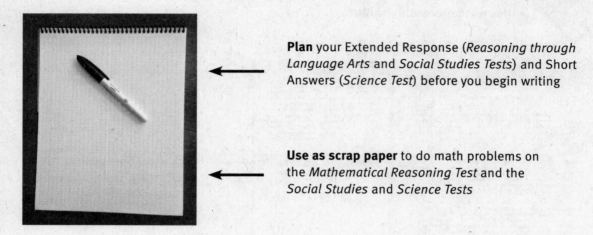

Plan your Extended Response (*Reasoning through Language Arts* and *Social Studies Tests*) and Short Answers (*Science Test*) before you begin writing

Use as scrap paper to do math problems on the *Mathematical Reasoning Test* and the *Social Studies* and *Science Tests*

Use three **onscreen test-tracking tools** at the top of the computer screen to

Test - Your Name   ⏱ Time Remaining 01:04:32
                                          ⬚ Question 32 of 50
                                          ⚑ Flag for Review

- **See how much time you have left:** *Time Remaining* shows how much time is left to complete each test.
- **Monitor your progress** through each test by viewing the *Question Line*. You can check how far you have progressed and how many more questions you need to answer. Budget your time carefully to allow for these writing tasks:
  - 45 minutes for the Extended Response at the end of the first section of the *Reasoning through Language Arts Test*
  - 25 minutes for the Extended Response at the end of the *Social Studies Test*
  - 10 minutes for <u>each</u> of the Short Answer questions that are interspersed with other questions in the *Science Test*
- **Click** on the *Flag for Review* if you are unsure of an answer. (You should never skip a question.) If you click on it, the flag will display in yellow and will be marked on the Review Screen.

At the end of each test, if you have time left, you can use the **Review Screen** to go back and review questions that you marked.

HOW TO USE THE CALCULATOR

You will use math skills throughout the *Science* and *Social Studies Tests* as well as on the *Mathematical Reasoning Test*. The following pages provide instruction about the calculator and other tools you will have access to on test day.

Calculation Tools

Calculator For most of the *Mathematical Reasoning Test* and portions of the *Science* and *Social Studies Tests*, you will be able to use either a hand-held or an on-screen version of the **Texas Instruments TI-30XS MultiView™ scientific calculator**. You can access the on-screen calculator by clicking on this icon. You can also take your own hand-held TI-30XS MultiView™ calculator to use on test day.

⊟ Calculator

If you forget how to use a specific calculator function, you will be able to access a *Calculator Reference Sheet* from the computer screen by clicking on this icon. That reference sheet is reprinted in the back of this book.

◩ Calculator Reference

Accessing the Symbol Selector Toolbar

On some fill-in-the-blank problems, you may need to use a symbol from the symbol selector toolbar. This is not available for all problems, but this icon shows up when you need the toolbar:

When you **click** on this icon, a new window will open up with these symbols:

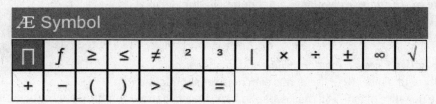

Click on a symbol to insert it in the correct place in an expression, equation, or inequality. When you are finished with the toolbar, **click** on the "X" at the top of the window to close the window.

If you do not know all of these symbols now, copy them on a piece of paper or in a math notebook. Use a GED® *Mathematical Reasoning Test* study resource to improve your familiarity with mathematical symbols.

Using the Wipe-Off Board

At the testing center, you will also be given a wipe-off board to serve as scratch paper. Even with all of the computer-based tools, you may still feel the need for some scratch paper to do the following:

- Write down the relevant numbers that you need to answer a specific question.
- Solve the problem by hand and use the calculator to check your work.
- Make a drawing or a diagram to help you picture a situation that is described in a problem.

At the testing center, you will be provided with a wipe-off board and dry erase marker, similar to the material shown at the right. Make use of the board throughout the test and ask for a new one if you feel that you need it.

Using the Texas Instruments TI-30XS MultiView™ Calculator

When you encounter questions in this book that involve math, you may use a calculator. We strongly encourage you to practice with the same calculator you will use on test day, namely the **TI-30XS MultiView™** calculator. Remember: You <u>do not have to</u> use the calculator to solve problems; only use it if it is relevant to the problem or if you believe it will be helpful.

Below is a picture of the hand-held version and some issues to keep in mind.

TI-30XS MultiView™ Calculator

- The <u>hand-held version</u> has an On/Off button at the lower-left hand side.

- To use the <u>on-screen version</u> of the calculator, **click** the calculator icon (see page xiii) to open the calculator in a new window. Use your mouse to **drag** the calculator to the side of the computer screen so that it does not cover the problem. When you are finished with a calculation, **click** on the "X" at the top of the window to close the calculator.

- When you are finished with a calculation, use the **_enter_** button. (There is no "equal sign" button on this calculator.)

- Use the **_white numeric keypad_** to enter numbers, the decimal point, and the negative sign (–) for a negative number such as −13 .

- The **_operation keys,_** on the right, allow you to add, subtract, multiply, and divide. (Use the minus sign here for subtraction; use the negative sign (–) on the keypad to indicate a negative number.)

- Use the bright green **_2nd button_** at the left of the calculator to activate the _2nd functions_ (in bright green) above the keys. Some of the main ones are square root, exponent, percent, and mixed number functions.

- The **_four arrows_** at the top right of the calculator allow you to move the **_onscreen cursor_** up, down, left, or right as needed. The **_delete_** key to the left of the arrows allows you to correct mistakes as you work.

- Every time you begin a calculation, press the **_clear_** button above the **_operation keys_** to clear the calculator's memory.

You are encouraged to purchase a hand-held version of the Texas Instruments TI-30XS MultiView™ calculator for practice as you work through this book. You can buy one at office or school supply stores or online.

Basic Calculator Functions

Look at the reproduction of the calculator below and follow the examples that demonstrate how to use the calculator's **operation keys**.

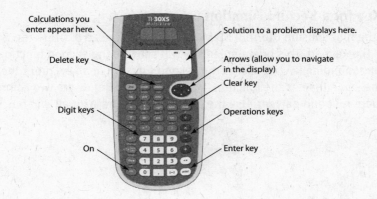

Calculations you enter appear here.

Delete key

Digit keys

On

Solution to a problem displays here.

Arrows (allow you to navigate in the display)

Clear key

Operations keys

Enter key

Example 1: Add $63 + 97 + 58 + 32 + 81$.

1. Always clear a calculator before starting a new computation. On the TI-30XS MultiView™, use the *clear* key.

   [clear]

2. Enter each number followed by the plus sign. As you type, the numbers and plus signs will appear on the calculator's screen. If you make a mistake, press *delete* to go back and reenter a number.

   63 [+] 97 [+] 58 [+] 32 [+] 81

3. Press *enter* to find the total.

   [enter]

The total, **331**, will appear on the right-hand side of the display:

331

Example 2: Find the difference between 15,789 and 9,332.

1. Always clear a calculator before starting a new computation.

   [clear]

2. Enter the greater number first, followed by the minus operator. **NOTE:** Use the minus key that is on the right side of the calculator with the other operation symbols. Don't use the (−) key at the bottom of the calculator; that key is used to enter a negative number.

   15789 [−]

3. Enter the number being subtracted.

   9332

4. Press the *enter* key to find the answer.

   [enter]

The answer **6457** will appear on the right-hand side of the display.

6457

Example 3: Find the product of 309 and 68.

1. Always clear a calculator before starting a new computation.

   [clear]

2. Enter the first number, followed by the multiplication operator. (The multiplication sign will appear in the display as an asterisk rather than an ×, but the *multiplication key* looks like an ×.)

   309 [×]

3. Enter the next number.

   68

4. Press the *enter* key to find the product.

   [enter]

The answer **21012** will appear on the right-hand side of the display.

21012

Example 4: Divide 12,456 by 12.

1. Always clear a calculator before starting a new computation.

   [clear]

2. Enter the number to be divided first, followed by the division operator.

   12456 [÷]

3. Enter the number you are dividing by.

   12

4. Press the *enter* key to find the quotient.

   [enter]

The answer **1038** will appear on the right-hand side of the display.

1038

Using the *2nd* Key for a Second Function

To access some of the functions on the TI-30XS MultiView™, you need to press the *2nd* key in the upper left corner of the keypad. This bright green key will activate the second function also shown in green above the corresponding key. To access the second function of a key, press the *2nd* key first—do not press it at the same time as the function key. High-lighted below are two commonly used second functions—square root and percent. Use the process shown here for all *2nd* function keys.

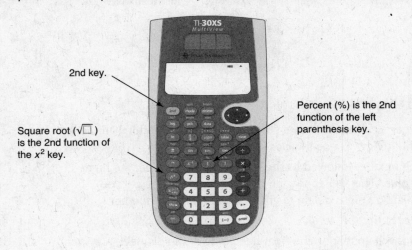

2nd key.

Square root (√▢)
is the 2nd function of
the x^2 key.

Percent (%) is the 2nd
function of the left
parenthesis key.

Example 5: Find the square root of 169.	**Keys to Press**	**On the Display**
1. Always clear a calculator before starting a new computation.	clear	
2. Recognize that square root is a *2nd* function over the x^2 key. Press the *2nd* key. (Note that the term *2nd* now appears in the upper left corner of the display.)	2nd	2nd
3. Next, press the x^2 key to activate the square root function in green over the key. You will see a blinking cursor under the square root.	$\sqrt{}$ x^2	√▢
4. Now that you have the square root function, enter the number. The number will appear under the square root symbol in the display.	169	√169 ▶
5. Press the *enter* key to find the square root. The answer, **13**, will appear on the right-hand side of the display.	enter	√169 13

Remember: For all *2nd functions*, (1) press the *2nd* key first to activate the *2nd* function, (2) press the key, and (3) enter the numbers.

Example 6: Find the part if you are given the percent and the whole. Find 10 percent of 500.

1. Always clear a calculator before starting a new computation.　　clear
2. Enter the number you want to find the percent of.　　500
3. Press the multiplication sign.　　×
4. Enter the percent number.　　10
5. Press the *2nd* key and then press the open, or left, parenthesis key to activate the percent function.　　2nd %(
6. Press the *enter* key to find the answer.　　enter

The answer, **50**, will appear on the right-hand side of the display. Ten percent of 500 is 50.

50

Example 7: Find the percent if you are given the whole and the part. What percent of 240 is 60?

1. Always clear a calculator before starting a new computation.

clear

2. Enter the part.

60

3. Press the division sign.

÷

4. Enter the whole.

240

5. Press the *2nd* key and then press the close, or right, parenthesis symbol. This tells the calculator to translate the answer into a percent.

6. Press the *enter* key to find the answer.

enter

The answer, **25%**, will appear on the right-hand side of the display. Sixty is 25% of 240.

25%

Decimal and Fraction Calculator Skills

Several important calculator keys are used to work with decimals and fractions.

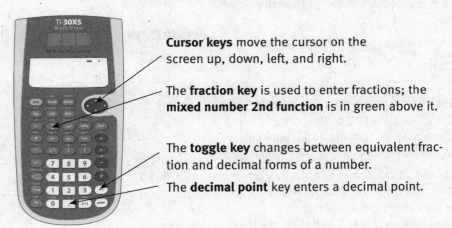

Cursor keys move the cursor on the screen up, down, left, and right.

The **fraction key** is used to enter fractions; the **mixed number 2nd function** is in green above it.

The **toggle key** changes between equivalent fraction and decimal forms of a number.

The **decimal point** key enters a decimal point.

Calculator **decimal operations** are performed in the same way that you use operations with whole numbers. You need to use the **decimal point key**⊙ under the 2 in the white **numeric keypad**. Practice with these examples:

To solve this problem...	Press these keys...	The right-hand side of the display reads...
$3.89 + 2.5$	3.89 + 2.5 enter	6.39
$5.2 - 0.78$	5.2 − .78 enter	4.42
0.9×15	.9 × 15 enter	13.5
$1.7 \div 2$	1.7 ÷ 2 enter	0.85

You will use several calculator functions to work with **fractions** and **mixed fraction operations**. First practice entering fractions and converting to decimals.

Example 8: Reduce $\frac{56}{448}$ to lowest terms and then convert to a decimal.

1. Clear the calculator.

__On the Display__

2. Press the $\frac{n}{d}$ button to enter a fraction. Enter 56 at the blinking cursor, in the numerator.

3. Use the down cursor key $\blacktriangledown$ to enter 448 in the denominator.

4. Press $\boxed{\text{enter}}$ to reduce the fraction to lowest terms, which appears on the right of your screen: $\frac{1}{8}$

5. To express the fraction as a decimal, press the toggle button: $\boxed{\blacktriangleleft\blacktriangleright}$. The decimal 0.125 appears on the right display.

A fraction answer may appear in the form of an improper fraction. In order to change an improper fraction to an equivalent mixed number, use the green 2nd function over this key:

Now practice operations with **mixed fractions** using the *2nd function* key.

Example 9: A plastic pipe is to be cut into pieces measuring $1\frac{7}{8}$ feet. The original pipe was $20\frac{5}{8}$ feet long. How many pieces can be cut from the pipe?

	Keys to Press	**On the Display**
1. Clear the calculator	$\boxed{\text{clear}}$	
2. Recognize that a mixed fraction is a green *2nd* function: $\cup\frac{n}{d}$ over the $\frac{n}{d}$ key. Press the $\boxed{\text{2nd}}$ key and the $\frac{n}{d}$ key. Note both a whole number and a blinking fraction cursor on the display.	$\boxed{\text{2nd}}$ $\frac{n}{d}$	■ ⊞
3. Enter the number being divided first—the whole pipe: $20\frac{5}{8}$. Enter 20, then follow the direction of the on-screen arrow and press the right arrow button to move to the fraction cursors. Enter 5 and then use the down arrow to enter the 8. Exit the fraction by pressing the right arrow again.	20 $\boxed{\blacktriangleright}$ 5 $\boxed{\blacktriangledown}$ 8 $\boxed{\blacktriangleright}$	$20\frac{5}{8}$
4. Press the division key. Then follow the same process with the second number: $1\frac{7}{8}$, starting with the 2nd function: $\boxed{\cup\frac{n}{d}}$	$\div$ $\boxed{\text{2nd}}$ $\frac{n}{d}$ 1 $\boxed{\blacktriangleright}$ 7 $\boxed{\blacktriangledown}$ 8 $\boxed{\blacktriangleright}$	$20\frac{5}{8}\div1\frac{7}{8}$
5. Press the $\boxed{\text{enter}}$ button for the solution. The answer 11 for **11 pieces** appears on the right side of the screen.	$\boxed{\text{enter}}$	$20\frac{5}{8}\div1\frac{7}{8}$ 11

As you read above, you can use the percent functions of your calculator to solve percent problems. You can also solve these problems by converting a percent to either a fraction or a decimal. Study the examples below.

Example 10: What is 25% of 120? Try both decimals and fractions.

<u>On the Display</u>

Change 25% to the decimal (.25), multiply times 120, and press enter. **30** is on the right of the display.

`.25*120        30`

Change 25% to the fraction $\frac{25}{100}$ using the $\boxed{\frac{n}{d}}$ key, multiply times 120, and press enter. **30** is on the right of the display.

`$\frac{25}{100}$*120     30`

Using either decimals or fractions, you can find that **30** is 25% of 120.

When you use the *percent 2nd* function, you don't have to convert the percent to a fraction or decimal. Practice this function below to multiply to find the **part** when you are given the rate (percent).

Example 11: What is 65% of $360?

Keys to Press	On the Display

1. Type the base, 360, and press the multiplication sign.

360 $\boxed{\times}$ `360*`

2. Type the rate (65). Press the 2nd function key and engage the percent 2nd function—over the $\boxed{(}$ key. Then press enter.

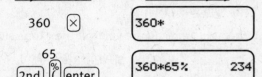

65
$\boxed{2nd}$ $\boxed{\%}$ $\boxed{enter}$ `360*65%      234`

The amount **$234** is 65% of $360.

You can use the percent function to divide to find the **base** when given the rate.

Example 12: Ned paid $150 for a stereo. The amount Ned paid was 20% of the original cost. What was the original cost of the stereo?

Keys to Press	On the Display

1. Enter the base, 150, and press the division sign.

150 $\boxed{\div}$ `150÷`

2. Enter 20 and press the 2nd function key and the $\boxed{(}$ key. Then press *enter*.

20
$\boxed{2nd}$ $\boxed{\%}$ $\boxed{enter}$ `150÷20%      750`

The original cost of the stereo appears on the right of the display: **$750.**

Expressions and Calculator Skills

The TI-30XS MultiView™ calculator, like most scientific calculators, uses algebraic logic, which means that it follows the correct order of operations.

You need to practice using a scientific calculator with algebraic logic. You can find out whether your calculator uses algebraic logic by running this simple test.

Press: 4 $\boxed{\times}$ 3 $\boxed{x^2}$ enter (Your calculator may have an equal sign instead of an *enter* button.)

If the display reads **36,** your calculator uses algebraic logic.

If the display reads **144,** your calculator does not use algebraic logic. You should find another calculator to practice for the GED® Test.

You can use a calculator to evaluate an expression that contains several operations.

Example 13: Find the value of the expression $2x^2 + 3x - 5$ when $x = -4$.

When you come to the variable x, enter −4 by pressing ⊟ 4. The ⊟ key is called the **change sign key**.

Press: ② 〔(⊟ ④)〕 x² ⊞ ③ ⊠ ⊟ ④ ⊟ ⑤ 〔enter〕

The right side of the display reads 15.

The value of the expression is **15**.

Expressions sometimes contain grouping symbols to show a different order of operations. You can enter grouping symbols on a scientific calculator. On the TI-30XS MultiView™, the grouping symbols 〔(〕 and 〔)〕 are found above the ⑧ and ⑨, respectively. When you enter the left, or open, parenthesis, 〔(〕, the calculator waits until you enter the right, or closing, parenthesis, 〔)〕, before it calculates what is inside the symbols.

Example 14: Find the value of the expression $2(x + 4) + \frac{5x}{3}$ when $x = 6$.

Press: 2 ⊠ 〔(〕 6 ⊞ 4 〔)〕 ⊞ 5 ⊠ 6 ÷ 3 〔enter〕.

The right side of the display reads **30**.

The value of the expression is **30**.

You can also use your calculator for only part of an expression.

Example 15: Find the value of the expression $\frac{3x + 6}{2} + \sqrt{225}$ when $x = 4$.

Substitute 4 for x in the first part of the expression and calculate the results by hand or using your calculator: $\frac{3(4) + 6}{2} = \frac{12 + 6}{2} = \frac{18}{2} = 9$.

Now use your calculator to find the square root of 225.

Press: 〔2nd〕〔x²〕 225 〔enter〕. The right side of the display reads 15.

Add the results of the two steps: $9 + 15 = \mathbf{24}$.

For more information about performing math skills on the GED® Test, consult a study resource for the *Mathematical Reasoning Test*, such as *Kaplan's GED® Test Mathematical Reasoning Prep*.

Pretest

The purpose of this pretest is to help you decide what you need to study to pass the actual GED® Science Test. You will use the pretest along with the explanations and the study planner that follows to determine what course of study works best for you.

This pretest is specially designed to make your study as efficient as possible. If you want to see what the actual GED® Science Test looks like, look at the *Practice Test* beginning on page 105.

1. **Take** the pretest:

   - **Science, pages 2–14**
     - Part I: Science Practices—10 Questions
     - Part II: Science Content—25 Questions
     - Part III: Short Answer

   Most of the questions are in multiple-choice format; one requires writing a short answer.

   - For the **multiple-choice questions**, you may fill in the circles next to the correct answers in this book, or you can write your answers on a separate piece of paper.
   - You can write your **short answer** on a computer or, if one is not available, on a sheet of paper.

   NOTE: Writing your responses on a computer is preferable because you will be composing your responses on a computer when you take the GED® test. However, if you do not have a computer available when you take these pretests, write your responses on paper so that you can evaluate your writing samples.

2. **Check** your answers with the *Pretest Answers and Explanations* that begin on page 16.

3. **Fill in** the *Pretest Study Planner* on page 20. These charts will allow you to target your problem areas so that you can study in the most efficient manner.

4. **Use the study planner** on page 20 to map out your work. Once you have completed your study, take the *Practice Test* on pages 105-117.

PART I: SCIENCE PRACTICES—10 QUESTIONS

Directions: You may fill in the circles next to the correct answers or write your answers on a separate piece of paper.

Questions 1 and 2 refer to the following passage.

For many years, scientists believed that all living things depended on sunlight for their energy. For example, human beings derive energy from food. Our food comes either from plants that require sunlight or from animals, which eat plants that require sunlight.

However, in the 1970s scientists discovered hot springs, called *hydrothermal vents*, in the ocean floor. These vents are miles below the surface of the ocean, far beyond the reach of sunlight. Yet these vents are surrounded by fascinating life forms, including giant red tube worms, eyeless shrimp, hairy-looking crabs, and communities of bacteria that grow like carpets on the ocean floor.

Those bacteria feed on minerals, like sulfur, that flow upward through the vents. The bacteria use a process called *chemosynthesis* to turn the minerals into nutrition. The bacteria, in turn, are eaten by many of the animals that live near the vents. Thus, those animals take in a source of energy that does not derive from sunlight.

1. Which of the following would be a good title for this passage?

    ○ A. "The Advantages and Disadvantages of Life Near Hydrothermal Vents"
    ○ B. "Hydrothermal Vents: A Potential Fuel Source for Our Energy-Hungry Economy"
    ○ C. "Hydrothermal Vents Suggest That Not All Life Is Solar-Powered"
    ○ D. "Major 20th-Century Advances in Oceanography"

2. Which of the following is a detail that supports the main idea of the passage?

    ○ A. Many scientists believe that all living creatures depend on sunlight for their energy.
    ○ B. Hydrothermal vents were not discovered until the 1970s.
    ○ C. The hairy-looking crabs are covered in structures that enable them to catch tiny particles of food.
    ○ D. No sunlight penetrates to the world of hydrothermal ocean vents.

Questions 3 and 4 refer to the following passage.

In a *radioactive* element like uranium, atoms give off some of their particles. In the 19th century, chemist Marie Curie discovered that the radioactivity of a compound depends on the amount of a radioactive element it contains.

Then Curie noticed something strange. Pitchblende, a compound that contains radioactive uranium, gives off more radiation than pure uranium. Curie wondered why that would be the case. She guessed that pitchblende might contain another element that was even more radioactive than uranium.

To find out, Curie and her husband isolated the elements that make up pitchblende. After isolating each element, they measured its radioactivity. As a result of this process, the Curies discovered that pitchblende contains a highly radioactive element, which no one had identified before. They named their discovery *polonium*.

3. Which of the following restates Marie Curie's hypothesis about pitchblende?

    ○ A. Pitchblende contains uranium.
    ○ B. Uranium interacts with the nonradioactive elements in pitchblende to increase its radioactivity.
    ○ C. Polonium was discovered by the Curies as a result of their experiment.
    ○ D. Pitchblende contains an element that is more radioactive than uranium.

4. Which of the following is a reasonable conclusion based on Curie's experiment?

    ○ A. Pitchblende is more radioactive than pure uranium because it contains polonium.
    ○ B. Polonium is only one of many reasons why pitchblende is more radioactive than pure uranium.
    ○ C. Marie Curie would become famous.
    ○ D. The Curies were not the first physicists to isolate polonium.

Questions 5 and 6 refer to the following passage.

The **ozone layer** is a part of the upper atmosphere with high concentrations of ozone, a form of oxygen. The ozone layer absorbs between 97 percent and 99 percent of the sun's medium-frequency **ultraviolet light**, which can cause skin damage and even skin cancers. For this reason, depletion of the ozone layer is a potentially global health risk. The ozone layer has been decreasing in thickness for decades due to atmospheric pollution. In particular, **chlorofluorocarbons** (CFCs), used in aerosol sprays and refrigerators, were so harmful to the ozone layer that a global ban was implemented in 1994, and production had almost entirely ceased by 2004. However, this ban was not effective; the hole in the ozone layer that appeared over Antarctica reached its largest recorded size in 2006.

5. Which evidence from the passage supports the conclusion that CFCs remain in the atmosphere for some time after their use?

   A. The ozone layer started thinning decades ago.
   B. The hole in the ozone layer reached its largest size after CFCs were banned from production and use.
   C. CFCs are used both in aerosols and as refrigerants.
   D. CFCs absorb medium-frequency ultraviolet light.

6. Which of the following additional pieces of evidence would best counter the author's opinion that the ban on CFCs was not effective?

   A. The ozone hole is not literally a hole but rather an area in which the ozone layer is depleted by more than 50 percent.
   B. While the ozone layer continues to thin, it is thinning at a rate much lower than it has in the past.
   C. Skin cancer rates near the equator, far from Antarctica, have not changed significantly since 1994.
   D. The CFC ban contains a few extremely narrow exceptions for uses where no suitable replacement exists, such as in fire-suppression systems on airplanes.

Questions 7 and 8 refer to the following text.

Adenosine triphosphate (ATP) is one of the most important chemicals for the function of the cells of all known living organisms. It stores and transports energy within and between cells. When a cell needs to use this energy, a chemical reaction releases it. Adenosine triphosphate and water can combine to remove either a **phosphate** (P_i) or **pyrophosphate** (PP_i) from the ATP, leaving **adenosine diphosphate** (ADP) or **adenosine monophosphate** (AMP) respectively.

Equation	Energy released (in kilocalories per mole)
$ATP + H_2O \rightarrow ADP + P_i$	7.3
$ATP + H_2O \rightarrow AMP + PP_i$	10.9

7. Which answer choice describes the process in the equation $ATP + H_2O \rightarrow AMP + PP_i$?

   A. Adenosine triphosphate is transported from one part of a cell to another.
   B. Adenosine triphosphate is broken down into adenosine monophosphate and a pyrophosphate, releasing energy.
   C. Adenosine monophosphate is broken down into water and a pyrophosphate, releasing energy.
   D. Adenosine monophosphate stores energy, which is transported to another cell.

8. Which of the following chemicals plays a role most similar to that of ATP?

   A. Lactase, which breaks down the lactose sugar found in milk for easier digestion
   B. DNA, which is found in the nucleus of every cell and contains instructions for the cell to manufacture proteins
   C. Hemoglobin, which allows red blood cells to carry oxygen
   D. Glycogen, which stores sugars that can be broken off in differing amounts when the body needs energy

Question 9 refers to the following information and table.

	P	P
w	Pw	Pw
w	Pw	Pw

	P	w
P	PP	Pw
w	Pw	ww

9. An equal number of seeds are produced from each of two pairs of flowers. One pair is a purebred pink plant with dominant pink genes (P) and a purebred white plant with recessive white genes (w). The other pair is made up of two hybrid plants, which are pink. The Punnett squares above show all possible combinations of alleles for the two pairs. If a seed is selected at random from the offspring of those two pairs, what is the probability that the selected seed will grow to be white?

- A. $\frac{1}{8}$
- B. $\frac{1}{4}$
- C. $\frac{3}{4}$
- D. $\frac{7}{8}$

Question 10 refers to the following graph.

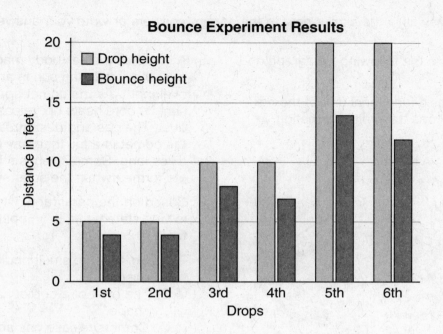

Bounce Experiment Results

10. A ball was dropped onto a surface from different heights, and the height of the first bounce of each drop was recorded. The graph above illustrates the initial heights and bounce heights of the six trials in the experiment. What was the average (arithmetic mean) difference between the drop height and the first bounce height, in feet?

○ A. $2\frac{1}{2}$

○ B. $3\frac{1}{2}$

○ C. 8

○ D. 21

Answers and explanations start on page 16.

PART II: SCIENCE CONTENT—25 QUESTIONS

Directions: You may fill in the circles next to the correct answers or write your answers on a separate piece of paper.

Question 1 refers to the following paragraph and diagram.

A neuron is the basic functional unit of the nervous system. Neurons transmit information throughout the body.

A Neuron

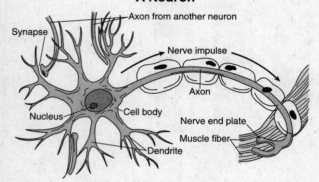

1. Which of the following is implied by the paragraph and the diagram?

     ○ A. Neurons are part of the endocrine system.
     ○ B. Oxygen is carried throughout the body by neurons.
     ○ C. Neurons transmit instructions regarding movement to muscles.
     ○ D. Nerve impulses travel from the axon to the cell body.

2. A comet is a small body made of ice and dust that orbits the sun in an elliptical, or oval, path. As the comet approaches the sun, its core heats up, releasing gas and dust. The gas and dust stream away from the comet in a tail that may be millions of miles long. Some scientists believe that comets formed when the solar system was born.

    Based on the paragraph, which of the following statements is an opinion rather than a fact?

     ○ A. Comets are small bodies of ice and dust.
     ○ B. The orbit of a comet has an elliptical shape.
     ○ C. Comets release gas and dust as they approach the sun.
     ○ D. Comets formed when the solar system was born.

3. In a photochemical reaction, light starts the reaction. Light can start a chemical reaction by exciting atoms and molecules, making them unstable and more likely to react with other atoms and molecules.

    Which of the following is an example of a photochemical reaction?

     ○ A. polymerization, in which long-chain organic compounds are formed from repeating units called monomers
     ○ B. fractional distillation, in which various petroleum products are separated out of crude oil
     ○ C. neutralization, in which an acid and a base react to form a salt and water
     ○ D. photosynthesis, in which green plants use the energy from sunlight to make carbohydrates from water and carbon dioxide

Questions 4 through 6 refer to the following chart.

Some Glands of the Endocrine System

Endocrine Gland	Hormone	Function
Pituitary gland	Growth hormone	Promotes bone and muscle growth
Ovary	Estrogen	Stimulates development of female secondary sexual characteristics
Testis	Testosterone	Stimulates development of male secondary sexual characteristics
Adrenal gland	Adrenaline	Increases heart activity, breathing rate, and blood flow to muscles for "fight or flight"
Thyroid	Thyroxine	Regulates metabolism and growth
Pancreas	Insulin	Regulates blood sugar levels

4. What is the function of the hormone thyroxine?

   ○ A. It controls female secondary sexual characteristics.
   ○ B. It controls male secondary sexual characteristics.
   ○ C. It speeds up the pulse and breathing rate for "fight or flight."
   ○ D. It helps control metabolism and growth.

5. People who have one form of the disease diabetes mellitus do not produce enough insulin. Based on the chart, what is the general effect of this disease?

   ○ A. stunted growth
   ○ B. excess growth
   ○ C. overproduction of estrogen
   ○ D. uncontrolled blood sugar levels

6. Paul, a child who was not growing as rapidly as he should, was given growth hormone to stimulate his growth. Paul anticipated that the hormone would enable him to reach an adult height of over six feet, even though his parents are both below average height. In fact, Paul's adult height was 5 feet 7 inches.

   What was wrong with Paul's thinking?

   ○ A. Growth hormone is only one of several factors that determine a person's adult height.
   ○ B. Growth hormone, when administered as a drug, does not affect a person's height.
   ○ C. In order to grow to over six feet tall, Paul would have had to take insulin, too.
   ○ D. In order to grow to over six feet tall, Paul would have had to take testosterone, too.

7. An emulsion is a mixture of two liquids whose particles are evenly scattered in one another without dissolving. Emulsions are unstable. After a time, the liquids separate.

   Which of the following is an emulsion?

   ○ A. tea with sugar
   ○ B. salt water
   ○ C. oil and vinegar salad dressing
   ○ D. food coloring and water

8. Earth science includes the study of Earth's atmosphere—the layer of gases that surrounds Earth—and Earth's hydrosphere—the oceans, rivers, lakes, and groundwater.

Which of the following scientists would be most likely to apply knowledge from a study of both the atmosphere and hydrosphere to his or her work?

○ A. a geologist who studies volcanoes and mountain formation
○ B. an astronomer who studies the planets of the solar system
○ C. a meteorologist who studies weather patterns and predicts weather
○ D. an ecologist who studies the distribution of populations of organisms

Question 9 refers to the following chart.

Organisms in a Food Chain

Role	Description
Producer	A green plant, which produces its own food using energy from sunlight
Herbivore	An animal that gets nutrients by eating plants
Carnivore	An animal that gets nutrients by eating other animals
Omnivore	An animal that gets nutrients by eating both plants and animals
Decomposer	An organism that gets nutrients from feeding on dead organisms and returns nutrients to the soil in the process

9. Earthworms break down large pieces of dead organic material in the soil. What role do earthworms play in the food chain?

○ A. They are producers.
○ B. They are herbivores.
○ C. They are carnivores.
○ D. They are decomposers.

Question 10 refers to the following graph.

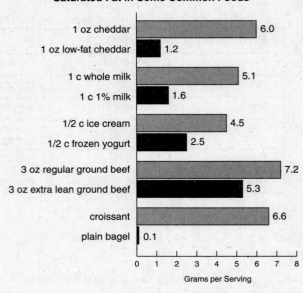

Saturated Fat in Some Common Foods

Food	Grams per Serving
1 oz cheddar	6.0
1 oz low-fat cheddar	1.2
1 c whole milk	5.1
1 c 1% milk	1.6
1/2 c ice cream	4.5
1/2 c frozen yogurt	2.5
3 oz regular ground beef	7.2
3 oz extra lean ground beef	5.3
croissant	6.6
plain bagel	0.1

10. Suppose a child's diet usually includes two servings of cheese, four servings of milk, one serving of ice cream or frozen yogurt, one serving of ground beef, and a croissant or bagel every day.

If the child's parent wanted to decrease the amount of saturated fat in the child's diet, which of the following actions would be most effective?

○ A. switch from regular to low-fat cheddar
○ B. switch from whole milk to 1 percent milk
○ C. switch from frozen yogurt to ice cream
○ D. switch from regular to extra lean ground beef

11. Torque is the ability of a force to produce rotation. The torque of any force is equal to the amount of the force multiplied by the distance from the pivot point to the point where the force is applied. For example, when you go through a revolving door, you are applying force as you push. The torque of your force is equal to the force you apply times the distance between your hand and the axis of the revolving door.

Which of the following actions would decrease torque as you go through a revolving door?

○ A. moving your hand closer to the center of the revolving door
○ B. moving your hand closer to the outer edge of the revolving door
○ C. pushing with two hands rather than one hand
○ D. leaning toward the door as you push to increase your force

Question 12 refers to the following graph.

U.S. Consumption of Energy by Source, 1997
(in common units of metric tons oil equivalent [TOE])

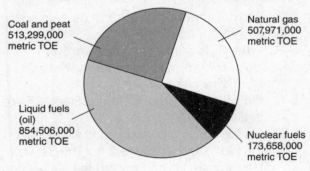

Coal and peat 513,299,000 metric TOE

Natural gas 507,971,000 metric TOE

Liquid fuels (oil) 854,506,000 metric TOE

Nuclear fuels 173,658,000 metric TOE

Source: World Resource Institute

12. Of the four energy sources shown, which two are the most similar in the proportion of energy they supply in the United States?

○ A. coal/peat and natural gas
○ B. natural gas and nuclear fuels
○ C. nuclear fuels and liquid fuels
○ D. liquid fuels and natural gas

Question 13 refers to the following paragraph and map.

In 1620, the eastern half of the United States was covered by virgin forest—forest that had never been cut down. Many parts of this region today are covered by second-growth forest—the ecosystem that eventually grows back after farmland is abandoned.

Virgin Forest of the United States 1620–1990

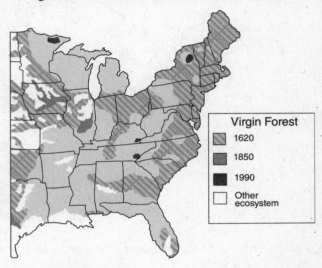

Virgin Forest
1620
1850
1990
Other ecosystem

Source: *National Geographic*

13. Which of the following conclusions is supported by the paragraph and the map?

○ A. The western half of the United States had far less forest cover in 1620 than did the eastern half.
○ B. As European Americans moved from the East Coast westward between 1620 and 1850, they cut down forests to build farms.
○ C. A number of relatively large areas of virgin forest remain in the eastern half of the United States today.
○ D. Today's second-growth forests in the eastern United States have fewer species of plants and animals than the virgin forest did.

Questions 14 and 15 refer to the following information and diagram.

The seasons occur because the axis of Earth is tilted. At different times of year, different parts of Earth get more hours of higher-intensity sunlight. As the diagram shows, summer begins in the Southern Hemisphere on December 21, when that hemisphere is tilted toward the sun.

Why Earth Has Seasons

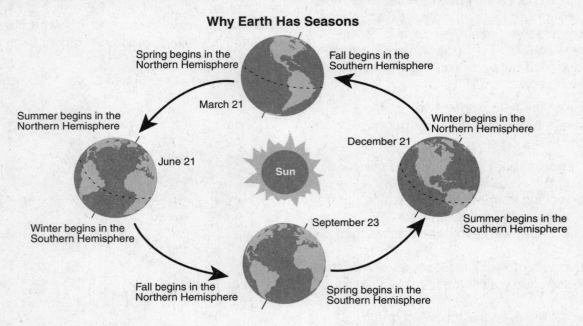

14. Which portion of Earth is tilted toward the sun on June 21?

○ A. the Southern Hemisphere
○ B. the Northern Hemisphere
○ C. the axis
○ D. the equator

15. Which of the following statements is supported by the information in the diagram?

○ A. Earth rotates once around its axis each and every day.
○ B. When it is summer in the Northern Hemisphere, it is summer in the Southern Hemisphere.
○ C. On March 21, the Northern Hemisphere is tilted toward the sun.
○ D. On the first day of spring and fall, neither the Northern Hemisphere nor the Southern Hemisphere is tilted toward the sun.

16. Ecologists use a tool called a quadrat when doing field studies of plant distribution. A quadrat is an open, four-sided structure about a meter square. It is placed on the ground, whether in a meadow, on a hillside, or at the beach. The ecologist then counts the plants of different species inside the quadrat. By using a quadrat, an ecologist can get a more accurate understanding of species distribution than by doing a random count.

Which of the following statements is a conclusion based on the given facts?

○ A. A quadrat is a tool used by ecologists.
○ B. A quadrat is a frame about a meter square.
○ C. To use a quadrat, the ecologist places it on the ground.
○ D. A quadrat makes plant distribution estimates more reliable.

17. According to Charles's Law, when the pressure of a gas remains constant, the volume of a quantity of gas varies directly with the temperature. In other words, as the temperature of a gas rises, the volume of the gas increases.

Which of the following graphs illustrates Charles's Law?

○ A.

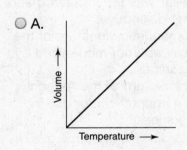

Temperature ⟶

○ B.

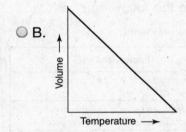

Temperature ⟶

○ C.

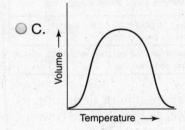

Temperature ⟶

○ D.

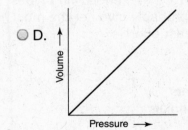

Pressure ⟶

18. At the beginning of the twentieth century, only three subatomic particles were known: protons, neutrons, and electrons. In the last half of the century, dozens of new particles were discovered using new technology. Machines called particle accelerators push particles to tremendous speeds. When two particles collide at high speed, they annihilate each other and new particles are formed.

Which of the following is not stated in the passage?

○ A. Protons, neutrons, and electrons are subatomic particles.
○ B. Atoms are composed of subatomic particles.
○ C. In particle accelerators, particles are pushed to very high speeds.
○ D. Particles that collide at high speed annihilate each other, forming new particles.

19. Density is the amount of matter, or mass, in a given volume of a substance. To find the density of an object, you divide its mass by its volume. A student wanted to find the density of a 3-cm cube of lead. First, she used a scale to find the mass of the cube. Next, she calculated the volume by multiplying 3 cm × 3 cm × 3 cm. Finally, she divided the volume by the mass to find the density of the lead cube.

Why was the density the student calculated inaccurate?

○ A. A scale cannot be used for finding mass.
○ B. Multiplying three sides of the cube will not give the cube's volume.
○ C. The student should have found the volume first.
○ D. The student should have divided the mass by the volume.

Questions 20 and 21 refer to the following information and diagram.

When the U.S. Mint had to design a new dollar coin to replace the old Susan B. Anthony dollar, it faced a problem. It wanted to design an appealing, distinctive golden-color coin that vending machines would recognize as an Anthony dollar, which looks like a quarter. Vending machines identify coins by their weight, size, and electromagnetic signature. They test a coin by passing an electric current through it and measuring the resulting magnetic field. Thus the new Sacagawea dollar coin had to be similar to the Anthony dollar in size, weight, and electromagnetic signature.

Size and weight were easy to imitate, but the electromagnetic signature was not. The Anthony dollar had a copper core covered by a silver-colored copper-nickel alloy. All the golden alloy sample coins had three times as much electrical conductivity as the Anthony dollar. Vending machines did not recognize them. Finally, metallurgists came up with the idea of adding manganese, which has low conductivity, to zinc and copper. The result was a coin consisting of 77 percent copper, 12 percent zinc, 7 percent manganese, and 4 percent nickel. The pure copper core was covered with a golden alloy of manganese, zinc, copper, and nickel. This golden coin has electromagnetic properties similar to those of the Anthony dollar, so it is recognized by U.S. vending machines.

20. It can be inferred from the passage above that an alloy is

  ○ A. a magnetic material
  ○ B. a material that stops electricity
  ○ C. a mixture of metals
  ○ D. the core of a coin

21. The U.S. Mint could have solved its technical problems with the Sacagawea dollar by making it out of the same metals as the Anthony dollar. Why did the people at the Mint decide against this?

  ○ A. The metals in the Anthony alloy were too rare and expensive to use in the new coin.
  ○ B. Like nickels, dimes, and quarters, the Anthony dollar was silver-colored and therefore not distinctive.
  ○ C. The electromagnetic signature of the Anthony coin was not recognized by vending machines.
  ○ D. The size and weight of the Anthony coin made it impractical for use in vending machines.

Question 22 refers to the following chart.

Types of Plants

Type	Characteristics
Annual	Completes life cycle in one growing season
Biennial	Completes life cycle in two growing seasons; flowers during second year
Perennial	Lives for years and flowers each year
Tender	Sensitive to cold (can be annual, biennial, or perennial)
Hardy	Can withstand frosts (can be annual, biennial, or perennial)

22. Marion has little interest in or time for gardening, yet she would like to have flowers in her front yard. Which of the following types of plants would probably give her the most flowers for the least effort?

  ○ A. annuals
  ○ B. biennials
  ○ C. tender plants
  ○ D. hardy perennials

Question 23 refers to the following information and diagram.

How a Reflecting Telescope Works

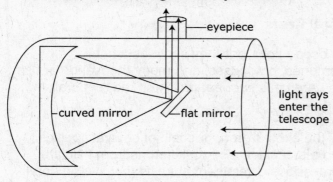

23. If the flat mirror were removed from this telescope, what would happen as a result?

○ A. Light rays would not enter the telescope.
○ B. Light rays would not reflect off the curved mirror.
○ C. A viewer could not see anything through the telescope.
○ D. A viewer could see only objects that were in focus.

24. The discovery of a new drug was once largely the result of trial and error, laboratory experiments, and clinical trials. Although these methods are still used, computer science is being applied to the drug discovery process to refine it and speed it up. For example, computers can analyze genetic material to locate genes that may hold promise in the development of new drugs. Computers can analyze data generated by lab experiments. Computer simulations can even help predict how a particular drug will work under specific circumstances.

What is the main reason that computers are now being used in the drug discovery process?

○ A. They enable scientists to abandon trial-and-error methods.
○ B. They help scientists analyze large amounts of data in a systematic way.
○ C. They have made laboratory experiments unnecessary.
○ D. They have made clinical trials unnecessary.

25. People planning to visit tropical countries may need to be vaccinated against disease. For example, two to four weeks before a trip, travelers should be vaccinated against typhoid fever. The vaccine is 50 to 80 percent effective. Additional precautions against typhoid fever include avoiding food and water that may be dirty.

If a traveler is vaccinated against typhoid fever two to four weeks before a brief trip to the tropics, which of the following best explains why he or she should take extra precautions against contracting the disease?

○ A. The typhoid fever vaccination is effective for only a few months.
○ B. The typhoid fever vaccination is only 50 to 80 percent effective.
○ C. The typhoid fever vaccination can cause soreness, fever, and headache.
○ D. Typhoid fever spreads only through air and water.

Answers and explanations start on page 16.

PART III: SHORT ANSWER

Directions: Read the selection and the writing prompt and answer the questions that follow.

Threats to Coral Reefs

Coral reefs cover a tiny percentage of the world's ocean floor, but they serve as a habitat for millions of marine species, including starfish, sea anemones, octopuses, and many thousands of fish species such as the clownfish. Some species, such as *Atergatis subdentatus*—the red reef crab—cannot survive in any other habitat besides coral reefs.

The hard substance that forms the reef is actually the exoskeleton, or shell, of several species of marine invertebrates. These invertebrates, called corals, make their exoskeletons from calcium carbonate ions dissolved in seawater. Despite the tremendous diversity of animals that live on coral reefs, corals themselves are delicate organisms. Even a minor environmental stressor, such as a slight change in pH or in water temperature, can cause corals to sicken and die. When corals die, the fish that depend on them for food also die. Scavenger species such as the red reef crab may experience a brief population boom, but once they have eaten all the dead fish, the scavengers die as well. In fact, dying corals wreak havoc with the entire reef ecosystem.

Writing Prompt

Carbon dioxide emitted into the atmosphere through the burning of fossil fuels by humans dissolves in seawater. This dissolved carbon dioxide lowers the pH of the water. Moreover, increasing levels of carbon dioxide in the atmosphere are causing ocean temperatures to increase.

Explain how the burning of fossil fuels by humans could affect the red reef crab (*Atergatis subdentatus*). Support your answer with multiple pieces of evidence from the passage.

The *Short Answer Scoring Guide* appears on page 19.

STOP

Congratulations! You have completed the GED® Science Pretest.

Reminder: your next step is to check your answers with the
Pretest Answers and Explanations and fill in the study
planner that follows those explanations.

PRETEST ANSWERS AND EXPLANATIONS

Part I: Science Practices, page 2

1. **C. "Hydrothermal Vents Suggest That Not All Life Is Solar-Powered"** The author's main point is that some of the life forms around hydrothermal vents derive energy from a source other than the sun. Choice (C) captures that idea. Choices (A) and (B) mischaracterize the subject matter of the passage, and choice (D) is far too broad.

2. **D. No sunlight penetrates to the world of hydrothermal ocean vents.** Only choice (D) supports the idea that some life forms derive energy from a source other than the sun. Choice (A) distorts the meaning of the first line of the passage. Choice (B) is true but does not serve to support this idea. Choice (C) is not stated in the passage.

3. **D. Pitchblende contains an element that is more radioactive than uranium.** A hypothesis is a guess made by a scientist before the scientist conducts an experiment. Before Marie Curie and her husband conducted their experiment with pitchblende, she guessed that pitchblende was more radioactive than pure uranium because pitchblende contained a radioactive element other than uranium. Curie already knew choice (A) to be true, so it was not a hypothesis she intended to test. Choice (B) is not stated in the passage. Choice (C) describes the outcome of the Curies' experiment, not their initial hypothesis.

4. **A. Pitchblende is more radioactive than pure uranium because it contains polonium.** As a result of their experiment, the Curies discovered that pitchblende contained polonium, a highly radioactive element. This suggests that Marie Curie's initial hypothesis was correct. The remaining choices are not supported by the passage.

5. **B. The hole in the ozone reached its largest size after CFCs were banned from production and use.** According to the passage, the hole in the ozone layer reached its largest size after CFCs were discontinued. The presence of CFCs that stayed in the atmosphere for years after use is a likely explanation for this phenomenon.

6. **B. While the ozone layer continues to thin, it is thinning at a rate much lower than it has in the past.** If the rate of ozone depletion has slowed significantly, it is likely that the CFC ban was at least partially effective.

7. **B. Adenosine triphosphate is broken down into adenosine monophosphate and a pyrophosphate, releasing energy.** The text describes this relation between ATP (adenosine triphosphate), AMP (adenosine monophosphate), and PP_i (pyrophosphate).

8. **D. Glycogen, which stores sugars that can be broken off in differing amounts when the body needs energy** Both glycogen and ATP store energy, and both can release different amounts of energy depending on the needs of the cell or organism.

9. **A. $\frac{1}{8}$** Because white is a recessive trait, a plant must have two white genes (ww) in order to be white. Of the eight possible outcomes illustrated in the Punnett squares, only one has this pair of genes.

10. **B. $3\frac{1}{2}$** The difference between the drop height and the first bounce height for the first drop was 1 foot. For the second, it was also 1 foot, and for the third, 2 feet. Find these differences for all the drops. The average of a set of items is the sum of the items divided by the number of items in the set. Thus, to find the average here, add all the differences and divide by the number of drops:

$$\frac{1+1+2+3+6+8}{6} = \frac{21}{6} = 3\frac{1}{2}$$

Part II: Science Content, page 6

1. **C. Neurons transmit instructions regarding movement to muscles.** Since neurons transmit information and the function of muscles is to move, it follows that neurons transmit instructions regarding movement to muscles. The paragraph and the diagrams show that all the other options contain incorrect information.

2. **D. Comets formed when the solar system was born.** Opinions are usually signaled by words like "believe," "think," or "feel." In this case, the last sentence of the paragraph states that scientists believe that comets formed when the solar system was born, showing that this is an opinion.

3. **D. photosynthesis, in which green plants use the energy from sunlight to make carbohydrates from water and carbon dioxide** The key element in a photochemical reaction is light. Of the options listed, only photosynthesis involves light.

4. **D. it helps control metabolism and growth** First, locate thyroxine in the "Hormone" column, then move along the row to the "Function" column to find the answer.

5. **D. uncontrolled blood sugar levels** The chart shows that insulin regulates blood sugar levels, so problems with insulin production will cause problems with blood sugar levels.

6. **A. Growth hormone is only one of several factors that determine a person's adult height.** Growth hormone alone does not determine height. A person's genetic make-up—the height of his parents and other family members—contributes, as do nutrition and the action of other hormones. Paul's expectations were therefore unrealistic.

7. **C. oil and vinegar salad dressing** This is an example

of an emulsion—two liquids mixed together but not dissolving. If you let oil and vinegar dressing stand, the oil will rise to the top. The other options are all solutions, which do not separate over time.

8. **C. a meteorologist who studies weather patterns and predicts weather** Knowledge gained from a study of the atmosphere and hydrosphere is closely related to the study of weather, which is influenced by both.

9. **D. They are decomposers.** Since earthworms are feeding on dead organic matter, which comes from dead organisms, they must be decomposers.

10. **B. switch from whole milk to 1 percent milk** The switch from whole milk to low-fat milk reduces fat intake by 3.5 grams/serving. While the difference in saturated fat per serving is greater in cheddar cheese than in milk, since the child drinks 4 servings of milk daily, this would be a reduction of 14 grams per day. The reduction from switching cheeses comes to 9.6 grams, since the child eats two servings of cheese per day.

11. **A. moving your hand closer to the center of the revolving door** Moving your hand closer to the center of the door decreases distance to the pivot point. Since the force remains the same in this case, when you multiply distance times force you will come up with a lower number, which indicates decreased torque.

12. **A. coal/peat and natural gas** Look on the circle graph for energy sources occupying wedges of approximately the same size. The only two that are about the same size are coal/peat and natural gas, indicating they provide about the same proportion of energy consumed in the United States.

13. **B. As European Americans moved from the East Coast westward between 1620 and 1850, they cut down forests to build farms.** The map shows, and the paragraph implies, that the virgin forests of the eastern United States were almost all cut down between 1620 and 1850. The paragraph further implies that the forests were cut down for farmland, which has since been abandoned. Based on this information, choice (B) is the only conclusion that is supported by the map and the paragraph. The map and the paragraph either lack support for or contradict the other options.

14. **B. the Northern Hemisphere** First, locate June 21 on the diagram, then examine the tilt of Earth. Note that at that time of year, the Northern Hemisphere tilts toward the sun, and it is summer there.

15. **D. On the first day of spring and fall, neither the Northern Hemisphere nor the Southern Hemisphere is tilted toward the sun.** According to the diagram, on March 21 and September 23, Earth's axis is tilted neither toward nor away from the sun, so neither hemisphere is tilted toward the sun. The remaining choices are not supported by the diagram.

16. **D. A quadrat makes plant distribution estimates more reliable.** This option is a conclusion, or a general statement, that is supported by all the details in the paragraph. The other options are specific details paraphrased from the paragraph.

17. **A.**

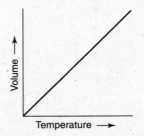

Charles's Law involves the relationship of a gas's volume and temperature. Since volume increases with increases in temperature, the first graph must be correct. Note that you can eliminate choice (D) immediately because it involves changes in pressure, and Charles's Law assumes that pressure remains constant.

18. **B. Atoms are composed of subatomic particles.** This is an assumption made by the writer of the paragraph. He or she does not explain this but assumes it is common knowledge. All the other options are statements made or strongly implied in the passage.

19. **D. The student should have divided the mass by the volume.** The paragraph states that density is calculated by dividing mass by volume. The student did the reverse, which is incorrect. All of the other steps the student followed were correct.

20. **C. a mixture of metals.** According to the passage, the Anthony dollar was made of a copper-nickel alloy, and the final Sacagawea dollar, of a manganese, zinc, copper, and nickel alloy. From these examples, you can infer that an alloy is a mixture of metals.

21. **B. Like nickels, dimes, and quarters, the Anthony dollar was silver-colored and therefore not distinctive.** The Mint wanted to replace the Anthony dollar with a distinctive coin—a coin that looked different from the coins already in circulation. Making the new coin out of the same metals as the silver-colored Anthony dollar would not accomplish this.

22. **D. hardy perennials** Hardy plants withstand frost, so they are more likely to survive than tender plants. Perennials come up and flower for many years. Therefore hardy perennials are likely to provide the most flowers with the least effort on the gardener's part.

23. **C. A viewer could not see anything through the telescope.** The function of the flat mirror is to redirect the light rays toward the eyepiece so the viewer can see the object in the telescope's sights. If the flat mirror were removed, the reflection of the object would no longer be visible through the eyepiece.

24. **B. They help scientists analyze large amounts of data in a systematic way.** The ability of a computer to process lots of data, far more systematically and quickly than a human being can, has helped speed up and refine the drug discovery process, although the older methods of running laboratory experiments and clinical trials are still also important.

25. **B. The typhoid fever vaccine is only 50 to 80 percent effective.** Because getting vaccinated against typhoid fever does not completely eliminate the traveler's chance of getting the disease, it makes sense that he or she should take extra precautions against contracting this food- and water-borne disease.

Part III: Short Answer, page 14

1. **Drafting Checklist** Check off each task that you performed. Give yourself a score of 0–3 based on how many checks you made.

   _____ I wrote a response based on my central idea (thesis statement).

   _____ I developed one to two well-developed paragraphs responding to the prompt.

   _____ In my response, I cited specific evidence from the text to support my central idea.

2. **Revising and Editing Checklist** Check off each task that you performed. Give yourself a score of 0–4 based on how many checks you made.

   _____ My piece was well organized.

   _____ My sentences were complete, clear, and correct.

   _____ I corrected subject-verb agreement, pronoun agreement, and verb tense errors.

   _____ I have corrected punctuation, capitalization, and spelling.

KAPLAN GED® SCIENCE TEST STUDY PLANNER

Take the Pretest, starting on page 1. Check your answers in the Pretest Answers and Explanations starting on page 16. Use the results to fill in the charts below so that you can target the areas that need the most work.

Part I: Science Practices, 10 Questions

Circle the *Question Numbers* that you answered correctly in the second column. Write the *Number Correct* in the third column. Compare your "number correct" to the "mastery" number in the fourth column. If you do not have time to review all of the *Science Practices* sections, target your study to the *Content Areas* in which you did not score at the mastery level.

Content Area	Question Numbers	Number Correct	Mastery/Total
Comprehend Science Presentations Pages 26–27	1, 2		**1 out of 2**
Use the Scientific Method Pages 28–29	3, 4		**2 out of 2**
Reason with, Express, and Apply Scientific Information Pages 30–33	5, 6, 7, 8		**3 out of 4**
Use Statistics and Probability Pages 34–35	9, 10		**2 out of 2**

Part II: Science Content, 25 Questions

Circle the *Question Numbers* that you answered correctly in the second column. Write the *Number Correct* in the third column. Compare your "number correct" to the "mastery" number in the fourth column. If you do not have time to review all of the *Science Content* sections, target your study to the *Content Areas* in which you did not score at the mastery level.

Content Area	Question Numbers	Number Correct	Mastery/Total
Life Science Pages 42–61	1, 4, 5, 6, 9, 10, 16, 22, 24, 25		**7 out of 10**
Earth and Space Science Pages 62–75	2, 8, 12, 13, 14, 15		**4 out of 6**
Physical Science Pages 76–91	3, 7, 11, 17, 18, 19, 20, 21, 23		**7 out of 9**

Part III: Short Answer

Compare your "number correct" to the "mastery" number in the fourth column. Study the *Short-Answer Content Areas* that need the most work. Target your study to the *Content Areas* in which you did not score at the mastery level.

Content Area	Score	Mastery/Total
Construct Short Answer Responses Pages 36–37	My score is _____ based on the Drafting Checklist, page 19.	**2 out of 3**
Construct Short Answer Responses Pages 36–37	My score is _____ based on the Revising and Editing Checklist, page 19.	**2 out of 4**

About the GED® Science Test

The GED® *Science Test* evaluates your ability to understand, interpret, and apply *science* information. You will have 90 minutes to answer 34 questions that are based on reading passages, graphics such as diagrams, tables, graphs, and maps, or a combination of the two.

You will need a minimum score of 150 to pass the *Science Test*, which is one of the four tests you will need to pass in order to earn a high school equivalency diploma.

Content Areas

Life Science (40%) topics include cell structures and processes, human body systems, health and nutrition, heredity and reproduction, genetics and DNA, evolution and natural selection, and the organization of ecosystems.

Earth and Space Science (20%) topics include the structure of Earth, plate tectonics, geological cycles and processes, renewable and nonrenewable natural resources, weather and climate, the solar system, and the universe.

Physical Science (40%) topics include atoms and molecules, properties and states of matter, chemical reactions, energy and work, motion and forces, waves, electricity, and magnetism.

Science Practices

In addition to testing your understanding of science passages and graphics, *Science Test* questions are based on your understanding of skills that are used in scientific study and investigation. These skills are called **Science Practices**, and they introduce this unit on pages 26–41. After you study these practices, you will reinforce them as you work through the unit. The science practices include the following:

- **Comprehend Scientific Presentations** to interpret passages and graphics.
- **Use the Scientific Method** to design investigations, reason from data, and work with findings.
- **Reason with Scientific Information** to evaluate conclusions with evidence.
- **Apply Concepts and Formulas** to express scientific information and apply scientific theories.
- **Use Probabilities and Statistics** in a science context.

Computer-Based Science Test Question Formats

You will work with six question formats on the *Science Test*. Many of the questions will be in the familiar multiple-choice format, but you will need to be acquainted with the other formats as well.

Multiple-choice questions have four options (A through D). You will **click** on the best answer.

GED® TEST TIP

If a multiple-choice question seems difficult, start by eliminating two choices that seem unlikely. Of the two that are left, select the one that makes the most sense. Remember, you can flag questions on the Science Test and come back to them if you have time.

A scientist concludes that frog and toad populations worldwide are in decline due to stratospheric ozone depletion, which results in more ultraviolet radiation from the sun reaching the earth's surface.

Which excerpt from the text most directly supports this conclusion?

- ○ A. "Embryos were examined at 12-hour intervals and the time from egg-laying to hatching was recorded for both groups."

- ○ B. "Ultraviolet radiation causes genetic mutations and abnormally slow growth rates in the embryos of most species of frogs and toads, thus negatively impacting survival rates."

- ○ C. "The control group was kept in a fully shaded enclosure, and UV levels were measured in both enclosures on a daily basis."

- ○ D. "For example, increased exposure to ultraviolet radiation may cause skin cancer in cattle."

Fill-in-the-blank questions will require you to **type** a word, phrase, or number in a box that appears on the screen.

Type your answers in the boxes:

A supplier of snapdragon seeds to the retail market is considering the genetics of snapdragon flower color. Red and white alleles display incomplete dominance; a plant with one red and one white allele will have pink flowers.

The seed supplier crosses a homozygous red snapdragon and homozygous white snapdragon. What is the likelihood that each seed produced will result in a certain flower color?

Red [ ] %
White [ ] %
Pink [ ] %
Yellow [ ] %

Drop-down questions give you the opportunity to **click** on the correct response to complete a statement.

The sugar glider is a pouched mammal, or [Select... ▾], that is native to [Select... ▾]. It is one of several gliding [Select... ▾] that behave similarly to flying squirrels. However, sugar gliders and flying squirrels are not close relatives; rather, their similar behavior is the result of [Select... ▾] evolution.

Hot-spot items consist of a graphic image. You will need to **click** on one or more "points" on the graphic as shown at the top of the next page.

The graph shows the relationship between an urban population of Peregrine Falcons and their primary prey species, feral rock pigeons, over time.

Select the area on the graph that represents the Peregrine Falcon population at time A.

To remove a point, place the arrow over the point and click the left mouse button.

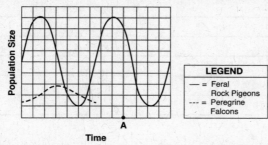

LEGEND

— = Feral
      Rock Pigeons
- - - = Peregrine
      Falcons

Time

A

Drag-and-drop items require you to **click** on a small image, words, or numerical expression and to **drag** and **drop** it in a specified location on the computer screen.

Identify the independent and dependent variable in the experiment.

Drag and drop the correct variable into each box.

Independent

Dependent

Variables:

Biomass of algae present in aquarium

Phosphorus concentration

Water temperature

Behavior of fish

Two *Short-Answer* items require you to **type in a text box with editing tools** to write a summary, create an experiment design, or explain how evidence supports a hypothesis or conclusion. Each Short-Answer question is expected to take about 10 minutes.

Desertification is a process in which relatively dry land such as grassland loses its plant and animal life and becomes a desert. Desertification can happen as a result of deforestation, overgrazing of livestock, and other human activities. It is currently happening in many regions around the world, including the Sahel region south of the Sahara desert.

Explain how desertification could disrupt the life cycle of *Adenium obesum,* a flowering plant native to the Sahel. Include multiple pieces of evidence from the text to support your answer.

Type your response in the box. This task may require approximately 10 minutes to complete.

✂ Cut ⎘ Copy ⎙ Paste ↶ Undo ↷ Redo

Math Problems on the Science Test

Many science investigations use mathematics. For that reason, there will be math questions on the GED® *Science Test*. You will focus on math skills in this book with the Science Practices lesson on pages 34–35.

Day	Noontime temperature in degrees Fahrenheit
April 15	58.0
May 15	65.4
June 15	76.9
July 15	88.2
August 15	87.3

$$C = \frac{5}{9}(F - 32)$$

What was the approximately temperature in degrees Celsius at noon on July 15?

You MAY use the calculator.

- A. 10.5
- B. 31.2
- C. 42.8
- D. 58.6

Solution:

Step 1: Write the equation $C = \frac{5}{9}(F - 32)$.

Step 2: Substitute 88.2 for F in the equation because the Fahrenheit temperature on July 15 was 88.2.

Step 3: Use the calculator to find the answer. $C = \frac{5}{9}(88.2 - 32) = 31.2$

Although you do not have to use a calculator, some problems will say: *You MAY use your calculator.* When you see that language, the calculator icon appears at the top of the screen. If you cannot remember how to use the calculator, you can open the online *Calculator Reference Sheet*.

You can **click** the links to **open, move,** and **close** both the online **Texas Instruments TI-30XS MultiView™** calculator and the Calculator Reference Sheet. You will want to move them on the computer screen so that they don't block the problem. Also remember that you will have an *off-line wipe-off board* that you can use as scratch paper.

Short-Answer Questions on the Science Test

Scientists and science students communicate about their work in writing. To reflect that, the GED® *Science Test* contains two Short-Answer items. You will focus on writing Short-Answers in this unit with the Science Practices lesson on pages 36–37.

The Short-Answer items are based on one passage, two passages, a graphic, or a combination. You will compose your answer in a text box similar to the one below.

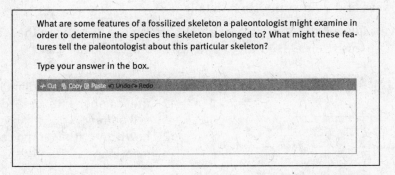

Read the prompt carefully and use the **online highlighter** to target specific facts and information that you will use in your response. Because this is a Short-Answer response, it is expected to be about one or two paragraphs long, with complete sentences and well-developed ideas.

An effective response must answer the questions and use specific information from the source materials. It should not be based on your opinions or personal experiences. Since the Short-Answer responses are worth up to 3 points each, take time to understand the question, plan your response, and choose several facts from the information to back up your position.

As with other writing tasks on the GED® Test, you have word processing tools that you can click on at the top of the toolbox that will allow you to do the following:

- **Cut** (remove extraneous ideas or correct mistakes)
- **Copy** and **Paste** (move words and ideas to improve your writing)
- **Undo** or **Redo** (use if your change your mind or want to restore)

SCIENCE PRACTICES

Comprehend Scientific Presentations

The GED® *Science Test* consists of questions based on science passages and graphics. To comprehend science presentations, you need to understand main ideas and their supporting details.

The **main idea** of a science presentation or graphic is its topic or the writer's point. Use this science diagram to practice finding the main idea.

Key Ideas

- *GED® Science Test* presentations consist of text, graphics, or a combination of the two.
- Understanding science presentations on the *Science Test* requires understanding the main idea or point.
- Main ideas in science materials are supported by specific facts, details, or evidence.

Dry Cell Battery

► What is the topic of this diagram?
  (1) the components of a dry cell battery
  (2) how a dry cell battery powers machinery

The correct answer is choice **(1)**. The diagram displays the different components (that is, the parts) of a dry cell battery. It does not show the process by which the battery actually operates or powers machinery, so choice **(2)** is incorrect.

Science writers support their main ideas with **details**, **facts**, and **evidence**.

Read the paragraph below and answer the question.

> Earthquakes can be classified as either surface earthquakes or deep-focus earthquakes. Scientists agree that surface earthquakes occur when rock in Earth's crust fractures to relieve stress. Deep-focus earthquakes originate from seismic activity more than 300 kilometers below Earth's surface. The causes of deep-focus earthquakes remain a subject of debate, but scientists believe they may be caused by the pressure of fluids trapped in Earth's tectonic plates.

► Which of the following details supports the main point of this paragraph?
  (1) The causes of deep-focus earthquakes remain a subject of debate among scientists.
  (2) Surface earthquakes are caused by stress in Earth's crust, while deep-focus earthquakes may be caused by pressure.

The correct answer is choice **(2)**. The main point of the paragraph is that earthquakes can be classified into two types based on their causes, and choice **(2)** provides supporting details that illustrate the differences between the two types. While **(1)** is mentioned in the paragraph, it is not a fact that supports the main point about the classification of earthquakes.

GED® TEST TIP

To answer GED® Science Test *questions based on a passage or graphic, ask yourself, "What is the main point? What evidence or details are used to support it?"*

PRACTICE 1

<u>Questions 1 through 3</u> are based on the passage below.

Despite the prevalence of type 2 diabetes, the causes of the disease remain somewhat uncertain. It is likely that some combination of genetics and lifestyle contributes to the development of type 2 diabetes. However, scientists have not fully determined the roles played by various lifestyle factors (such as diet and exercise).

For Americans, one contributing factor may be high sugar consumption. Sugar from food is broken down and absorbed into the bloodstream, and insulin is required for the body to be able to use that sugar. In a study of individuals 18–25 years old who consumed more than the recommended amount of sugar daily, it was shown that the majority had significantly elevated levels of glucose (that is, sugar) in their blood but normal levels of insulin. In other words, these subjects could not produce enough insulin to allow their bodies to use the amount of sugar they were consuming. Elevated blood glucose levels may put individuals consuming high amounts of sugar at higher risk of developing type 2 diabetes.

1. Which one of the following is the topic of the entire passage?

A. sources of sugar in Americans' diet
B. the role of insulin in metabolizing sugar from food
C. the causes of type 2 diabetes
D. how to prevent type 2 diabetes

2. Which of the following is the main idea of the first paragraph?

A. It is likely that sugar consumption contributes to the development of type 2 diabetes.
B. It is likely that genetics plays a role in the development of type 2 diabetes.
C. Researchers have discovered the causes of type 2 diabetes.
D. The causes of type 2 diabetes are not fully understood.

3. The main idea of the second paragraph is that high sugar consumption may put individuals at greater risk of developing type 2 diabetes. Which of the following details from the second paragraph supports that main idea?

A. Sugar from food is absorbed into the bloodstream.
B. A study of 18–25 year olds showed that a majority did not produce enough insulin to offset the high amounts of sugar they were consuming.
C. A study of 18–25 year olds showed that high sugar consumption interacted with genetic factors in a majority of those individuals in order to suppress insulin production.
D. It has not been proven that sugar is a contributing factor to the development of type 2 diabetes.

Question 4 is based on this graphic.

How Topography Contributes to Precipitation

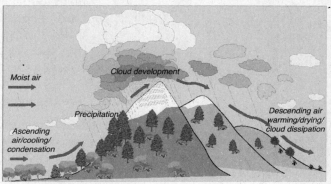

Source: U.S. Geological Survey

4. Which statement correctly describes the process depicted in the graphic above?

A. As moist, flowing air encounters rising elevations, it cools, which causes condensation, a stage that precedes precipitation and cloud development.
B. Once above the tree line, flowing air is likely to slow down and stop moving, and then collect in the form of snow.
C. Clouds dissipate before encountering mountain peaks.
D. Moist air flows from the west, while drier air usually flows from the east.

Answers and explanations begin on page 92.

SCIENCE PRACTICES

Use the Scientific Method

The **scientific method** is a set of techniques that scientists use to investigate observable facts and occurrences and to acquire new knowledge. Here are the steps in the scientific method:

1. **Observe a phenomenon** and **formulate a question** about it. The scientific method starts with a **question** about something that you observe. Formulate the question about something that you can measure.
2. **Collect data** about the phenomenon you are studying. Scientific study is founded on **data**, or observable facts, which are used to describe a phenomenon.
3. **Form a hypothesis**. A **hypothesis** is an educated guess about the answer to your question.
4. **Test the hypothesis through an experiment**. Your experiment should be a fair test of the hypothesis. You may need to adjust the experiment. You would do so by changing only one factor at a time while **controlling** other factors. You should also repeat the experiment to make sure the first results are valid.
5. **Draw a conclusion** about the hypothesis based on the experiment. When the experiment is complete, you may conclude that your hypothesis was supported by the data or that it was not, in which case you may formulate a new hypothesis.

Key Ideas

- The scientific method is used to investigate events and to acquire knowledge.
- Scientists follow a series of procedures involving observing, collecting information, and forming a hypothesis.
- After the hypothesis has been tested in an experiment or study, scientists draw a conclusion.

ON THE GED® TEST

The GED® Science Test may present an experiment and ask you to answer multiple-choice questions or to write a Short Response to a question about it.

Read about scientific observation and answer the question below.

Scientists observed unusual plant and algae growth in a pond. They sampled the water and also discovered very high concentrations of bacteria. Significant increases in the growth of plants, algae, and bacteria in ponds are often caused by an excess of phosphates and nitrates in the water. The pond was fairly close to neighboring farmland, and two streams carried water from the farm to the pond.

▶ What could be a sound hypothesis about the growth in the pond?
   (1) Runoff from the neighboring farm may be carrying excessive phosphates and nitrates from fertilizers into the pond.
   (2) Proximity to farmland is the cause of plant and algae growth in ponds and other bodies of water.

If you chose **(1)**, you are correct. That hypothesis is an educated guess about the reason for the unusual plant and algae growth in the pond. It could be tested by an experiment that compares samples from the pond water to samples from streams coming from neighboring fields. Choice **(2)** is an assertion that is very general and cannot be measured in this specific situation.

The phenomenon you are studying is called the **dependent variable**. A factor that you believe might be affecting that phenomenon is called the **independent variable**. In the example above, the unusual plant and algae growth would be the dependent variable. The runoff from the neighboring farm would be the independent variable.

PRACTICE 2

Questions 1 through 3 are based on this passage.

A majority of teenagers develop acne, but scientists still struggle to explain its cause. It has long been thought that bacteria play a role, although until recently it was assumed that role was purely detrimental—contributing to acne. However, a team of researchers began to wonder whether different strains of bacteria might impact acne in different ways.

The research team studied 49 individuals with acne and 52 individuals without acne, and the researchers collected samples of bacteria from the nasal pores of all those individuals. The researchers found that some combinations of bacterial strains were highly likely to be found in clear-skinned individuals, while other combinations were highly likely to be found in individuals with acne.

After carefully analyzing their data, the scientists concluded that, while some bacterial combinations likely contribute to acne, other bacterial combinations may actually help to ward it off. The researchers suggested that, if further studies confirm these findings, we may want to treat acne by encouraging the growth of helpful bacteria.

1. Use the boxes below to identify the researchers' independent and dependent variables.

Independent variable	Dependent variable

acne symptoms	combinations of bacteria

teenagers	treatments for acne

2. What was the researchers' hypothesis?

A. Combinations of bacteria are a major cause of acne.
B. Different kinds of bacteria may impact acne differently.
C. We may want to change the way we treat acne, treating it by encouraging the growth of beneficial bacteria.
D. Some combinations of bacteria may actually help ward off acne.

3. What conclusion did the researchers reach based on their data?

A. Combinations of bacteria are a major cause of acne.
B. Acne sufferers have more types of bacterial strains in their facial pores than do non-sufferers.
C. The way we currently treat acne is misguided.
D. Some combinations of bacteria may actually help ward off acne.

Question 4 is based on the following information.

Suppose that you notice your right knee hurts every time you play softball. You suspect that one of the movements involved in playing softball is causing your knee to hurt, but you are not sure which movement is the culprit. You decide to do a scientific investigation to find out more.

4. Match each of the following steps of the scientific method with a phase of your investigation (listed below the table).

a) Form a hypothesis.	
b) Design a test for your hypothesis.	
c) Collect data to test your hypothesis.	
d) Form a conclusion based on the data from your test.	

i) You make a list of each of the movements involved in softball. In the off season (when you are not playing entire games), you plan to perform each movement several times without performing the others.

ii) Based on the data you collected in your experiment, you think it is likely that stopping suddenly after running a short distance is indeed the cause of your knee pain.

iii) Based on your experience, you make a guess about which of the movements involved in playing softball puts the greatest stress on the knees. You suspect that it may be stopping suddenly after running a short distance.

iv) After performing each movement in isolation, record how your knee feels. Let your knee recover between tests of each type of movement.

Answers and explanations start on page 92.

SCIENCE PRACTICES

Reason with Scientific Information

Key Ideas

- Reasoning with scientific information requires citing specific evidence to support a conclusion.
- In some cases, an existing theory can be challenged by new data or evidence.
- One of the ways scientists use information is in making predictions.

Some GED® *Science* questions require recognizing or citing specific evidence to support a conclusion. Another type of question may ask you to judge whether a **conclusion** or a **scientific theory**—a substantiated explanation of the natural world—is challenged by particular data or evidence.

Use the graph below to practice scientific reasoning.

Rates of Infant Mortality, 1940–2009

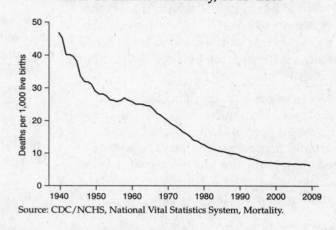

Source: CDC/NCHS, National Vital Statistics System, Mortality.

► Which conclusion is supported by the data on the graph?
(1) The rate of infant deaths in the United States experienced its sharpest decline between roughly 1940 and the late 1950s.
(2) In each year between 1940 and 2009, there were fewer infant deaths than in the year before.

The correct answer is choice **(1)**. The graph shows that the rate of infant mortality decreased most sharply between the years of 1940 and the late 1950s. After the late 1950s, it continued to decrease, but more gradually. Choice **(2)** is not a true statement based on the graph: around 1960, there was an uptick in the rate of infant deaths.

Other questions will ask you to make a **prediction** based on evidence or data that the test provides to you. Based on the **trend** observed, scientists use data to predict, or forecast, what they think may happen in the future.

► Which of the following predictions is based on the graph above?
(1) Since there has not been an increase in infant deaths since 1960, there will likely be such an increase sometime soon.
(2) The rate of infant deaths is unlikely to experience sharp declines in the near future.

Choice **(2)** is correct: the line on the graph shows the trend in infant mortality has been one of very gradual decrease since the 1950s. A good prediction based on that pattern would be that the trend of gradual decline is likely to continue. The graph shows a downward trend, but gives no information to suggest a future increase, so choice **(1)** is incorrect.

PRACTICE 3

1. Inertia causes an object to resist changes in its state of motion. In other words, inertia causes an object at rest to resist any attempt to set it in motion. Similarly, inertia causes an object in motion to resist any attempt to stop its motion. Objects with greater mass have greater inertia.

   These figures represent the mass of two objects:

   Brick: 100 grams
   Block of wood: 70 grams

   Which of the following is supported by the information above?

   A. It would require more effort to break the brick than to break the block of wood.
   B. If both objects were currently sitting still, it would require more effort to push the block of wood across the floor than it would to push the brick across the floor.
   C. If both objects were currently sitting still, it would require more effort to push the brick across the floor than it would to push the block of wood across the floor.
   D. The brick would absorb water more readily than would the block of wood.

2. In the last several decades, the spider population has exploded on the island of Guam: parts of the island have as many as 40 times more spiders than nearby islands do. One scientist has concluded that the explosion in the Guam spider population is due to an increase in the population of an invasive species of brown tree snake. The snake was introduced into Guam in the 1940s but was not introduced into the neighboring islands. The brown tree snake preys on birds.

   Which one of the following, if true, makes the scientist's conclusion more likely?

   A. The birds that the brown tree snake eats are the primary predators of spiders on Guam.
   B. The brown tree snake is typically introduced into islands via ships carrying tourists. Guam and the islands nearby have long been popular tourist spots.
   C. Brown tree snakes eat spiders as well as birds.
   D. In the rainy season, the island of Guam can have more than 40 times as many spiders as it did ten years ago.

Questions 3 and 4 are based on the following passage:

Melting ice sheets in Greenland and Antarctica have the potential to contribute significantly to rising sea levels in the next century. Some ice sheets melt more quickly than others, and scientists have wondered why. A team of researchers recently used data from both satellites and radar to study the composition of many of the ice sheets in Greenland and Antarctica. They found that some of the ice sheets formerly thought to sit on rock actually sit on water. This finding could be significant because it may be the case that ice sheets sitting on water tend to melt more quickly than those sitting on rock.

3. Which of the following is a prediction scientists might make based on the information above?

   A. If large areas of ice sheets sit on rock, the rising of sea levels may proceed more quickly than had previously been predicted.
   B. If large areas of ice sheets sit on water, the rising of sea levels may proceed more quickly than had previously been predicted.
   C. Ice sheets in Greenland will likely melt more quickly than ice sheets in Antarctica.
   D. All the ice sheets that are melting more quickly will be found to be sitting on water.

4. A scientist predicts that the ice sheets sitting on water will collectively discharge more water into the ocean than will those sitting on rock. Which of the following facts, if true, might weaken that prediction?

   A. Most of the ice sheets sitting on water are covering inland lakes with no access to the ocean.
   B. Water sitting under ice sheets flows directly into the ocean.
   C. Ice in a glass of water will melt even if the room is very cold.
   D. Radar used alone is an unreliable way to assess the composition of ice sheets.

Answers and explanations start on page 93.

SCIENCE PRACTICES

Express and Apply Scientific Information

Scientific information can be expressed in different forms. On the GED® *Science Test*, you may be asked to find relationships among science passages, graphics, formulas, or equations.

Scientific equations for **chemical reactions** often use these symbols:

Symbol	Meaning
+	Positive symbol separates two or more **reactants** or **products** from one another.
→	Yield symbol separates reactants from products and shows the reaction direction.
⇆	Reversible reaction symbol indicates that the reaction can proceed in both directions.

For example, here is the general chemical formula for what happens when carbon (C) is burned:

$$C + O_2 \rightarrow CO_2$$

▶ Which statement describes the process in the formula?
   (1) Carbon combines with oxygen to produce carbon dioxide.
   (2) Carbon creates oxygen, which takes on another oxygen atom in order to produce carbon dioxide.

The correct answer is statement **(1)**. In this case, carbon and oxygen (O_2) combine without losing any of their components. The result is carbon dioxide, a molecule made up of one carbon atom and two oxygen atoms. (The prefix *di-* means "two," so *carbon dioxide* means "a C and two Os.") The plus sign on the left-hand side of the formula indicates that carbon and oxygen are separate reactants, not that carbon creates oxygen. Thus, statement **(2)** is incorrect.

Other questions may ask you to understand a science concept and **relate** it to a specific situation.

The term *desertification* describes a chain of events in which so much soil erodes from land that the land can no longer support plant or animal life. The lack of plant life allows for further soil erosion, making the land even more barren. It is very difficult to reverse desertification.

▶ Which of the following could be an example of the early stages of desertification?
   (1) In a certain valley, overgrazing has nearly eliminated plant life. This lack of vegetation has led to rapid soil erosion.
   (2) In a certain valley, the climate is arid, and soil erosion has occurred when the infrequent rains arrive. Farmers have devised an irrigation system to grow crops and thus reverse the rate of soil erosion.

Choice **(1)** is correct. Soil erosion is the cause of desertification, so the valley may be in the early stages of desertification. In choice **(2)**, farmers have found a way to combat erosion, so this valley does not appear to be undergoing desertification.

Key Ideas

- Scientific information can be conveyed in multiple forms: in words, graphics, or formulas.
- Scientific formulas use numbers, letters, and symbols to represent a relationship or process.
- An important science reasoning concept is the ability to apply a scientific concept to a different situation.

ON THE GED® TEST

When you are given a science concept and asked which one of the choices is the best example, carefully eliminate the three that do not have all the same characteristics.

PRACTICE 4

Questions 1 through 4 are based on the information below.

Imagine a substance (such as salt or sugar) dissolved in a liquid (such as water or alcohol). The liquid in which the substance is dissolved is called the *solvent*. *Osmosis* is the diffusion (movement) of a solvent across a semipermeable membrane (a barrier that allows some substances to pass through it). The solvent moves from the side of the membrane with less dissolved material to the side of the membrane with more dissolved material. The result of osmosis is an equilibrium: the state in which the rate at which the solvent flows across the membrane at the same rate in both directions.

Gillian conducted an experiment to see how quickly various liquids with a specific amount of sugar dissolved in them would undergo osmosis. She used vats of the same size with semipermeable membranes separating one side of the vat from the other, and she put equal quantities of various liquids in both sides:

Container Used for Studying Osmosis

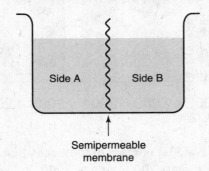

Semipermeable
membrane

1. Gillian used one of the vats to test the rate of diffusion of liquid acetone in the process of osmosis. What did she most likely put on the two sides of the semipermeable membrane in that vat?

	Side A	Side B
A.	Pure acetone	Sugar in a glass container, submerged in acetone
B.	A 50 percent solution of sugar in acetone	A 50 percent solution of sugar in acetone
C.	Pure acetone	A solution of sugar in acetone
D.	Pure acetone	Pure acetone

Gillian's experiment yielded the following results.

Solvent	Time Required to Reach Equilibrium
Water	20 minutes
Acetone	25 minutes
Acetic acid	18 minutes
Formic acid	15 minutes

2. Based on the table above, which solvent had the highest rate of diffusion?

A. water
B. acetone
C. acetic acid
D. formic acid

3. Based on the table above, calculate the average (mean) time required for the solvents to reach equilibrium. [   ]

4. Osmosis is the reason why it is unhealthy and potentially dangerous to drink seawater. If you drink seawater, which contains a high concentration of salts and other dissolved material, some of the dissolved material will be absorbed into your bloodstream, causing your blood to have a higher-than-normal concentration of dissolved material. As that blood circulates through your body, water will move from your body's tissues into your blood vessels, causing your tissues to lose water and dry out.

Fill in the blank with one of the choices: Based on the information above, your tissues would begin to lose water and dry out when your blood has a level of dissolved material [Select... ▾] that of your body's tissues.

- greater than
- less than
- equivalent to

Answers and explanations start on page 93.

SCIENCE PRACTICES

Use Statistics and Probability

Key Ideas

- A measure of central tendency is used to summarize data.
- Probabilities are used to make predictions.
- Combinations and permutations are used to calculate numbers of ordered and unordered arrangements, respectively.

ON THE GED® TEST

When you need to compute on the GED® Science Test, a calculator symbol with the word "Calculator" will appear on the toolbar at the top of your screen. Click on it to open the online calculator.

Because scientists often need to perform calculations, you will do some math on the GED® *Science Test*. This math work will include the following:

- Central tendency—average (mean), median, mode, and range
- Independent and dependent probabilities
- Counting techniques for combinations and permutations

Scientists use **measures of central tendency** (mean, median, mode, and range) to summarize many pieces of data with one number.

Use the graph below to answer a question about central tendency.

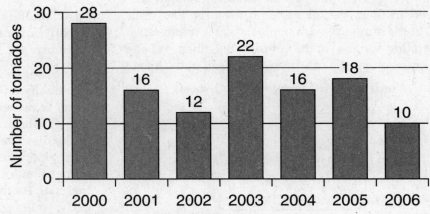

Annual Tornadoes, 2000–2006, Goodland (Kansas) 19-County Warning Area

Source: National Oceanic and Atmospheric Administration

▶ Calculate the mean (arithmetic average) number of tornadoes that struck the Goodland area per year in the years 2002 through 2005.

To find the mean of a set of quantities, sum the quantities and divide by the number of items in the set. The list from 2002 to 2005 is 12, 22, 16, and 18. The sum of those numbers is 68. Divide by the number of items in the list (4), and the result is **17**.

Scientists frequently use data to investigate the **probability** that an event will happen.

PRACTICE 5

Questions 1 through 4 are based on the following information.

Metabolism is a set of chemical processes that occur in the tissues of living organisms. One example of a metabolic process in animals is the breaking down of carbohydrates from food into substances the body can store. Another example is the transformation of those same substances into energy that the animal can use. The *rate of metabolism* describes the speed at which these processes take place. Metabolic rate varies among different species. The graph below compares several animal species by both average metabolic rate and average body weight.

Metabolic Rates of Seven Species

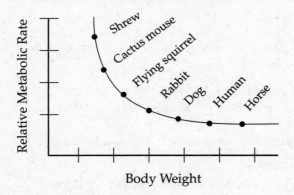

Body Weight

1. Of the species in this graph, which has the median body weight? [   ]

2. Of the species in this graph, which has the median metabolic rate? [   ]

3. Imagine that you could calculate the average (mean) of metabolic rates of all the animal species in this graph. Now imagine that the shrew were removed from the graph and that you recalculated the average of the remaining species. Without the shrew, the new average metabolic rate would be [Select... ▾].

   - higher than the previous average
   - lower than the previous average
   - about the same as the previous average

4. Adult elephants weigh more than adult horses. Based on the graph above, what would you predict would be true of elephants?

   A. Their metabolic rate would resemble that of cactus mice, which, like elephants, live in warm climates.
   B. Their metabolic rate would be equivalent to that of horses.
   C. Their metabolic rate would be slightly lower than that of horses.
   D. Their metabolic rate would be significantly higher than that of horses.

5. Growing the same crop on a field year after year can cause crop yields to decline as the soil becomes depleted and insect populations become firmly established. Crop rotation, or growing different crops in different years, is one way to avoid these problems. However, discovering the most effective rotation of a number of different crops is difficult, because there are so many possible orders in which to grow them and testing any given crop rotation takes several years.

   For example, imagine a proposed rotation of corn, peanuts, onions, beets, and carrots, with a different crop grown each year for five years. How many different orderings of these five crops are possible?

   A. 15
   B. 25
   C. 120
   D. 125

Answers and explanations begin on page 93.

SCIENCE PRACTICES

Construct Short–Answer Responses

Key Ideas

- You can take about ten minutes to plan and write each of the two Short-Answer responses on the GED® Science Test.
- You may be asked to respond to a question about a passage, graphics, or both.
- You might also be asked to write a design for an experiment.

GED® TEST TIP

Each Short-Answer response is worth up to 3 points. You can improve your score when you use two or three specific facts, details, or pieces of evidence from the passage in your response.

The GED® *Science Test* will require you to write *two* written responses to a passage, graphic, or combination of the two. Pages 23 and 25 have more information about Short-Answer responses on the GED® *Science Test*.

You could be asked to complete one or both of the following types of writing tasks within a writing text box that will appear on your computer screen:

- **Cite specific evidence** to support inferences, conclusions, or analyses of scientific information.
- **Design a scientific experiment** to test a hypothesis. As you read in Lesson 2: Use the Scientific Method on page 28, this involves how data are collected, tested, and evaluated.

A response to a question based on text, graphics, or a combination of the two should contain the following:

- A complete and well-developed explanation
- Specific facts, details, or evidence from source material

A plan for a scientific experiment should include the following:

- A clearly stated hypothesis
- A well-formulated design of how the experiment would be conducted
- A logical method to collect the data
- Sound criteria for evaluating the results in relation to the hypothesis

Since each of the Short-Answer responses are worth more than individual multiple-choice questions, they are well worth your time to carefully plan, organize, and write. You should budget 10 minutes for *each* Short-Answer question out of the total 75 minutes on the *Science Test*.

Practice this five-step process with the Short-Answer response questions on the next page and throughout the science units in this book.

1. **Read the question** carefully and mentally put it in your own words.
2. **Develop a thesis statement** that (a) explains your position or (b) describes your experiment design.
3. Reread the information that is provided and use the online highlighter to **emphasize the facts, details, and evidence** you will use in your response.
4. Use the provided wipe-off board to **plan your response**.
5. **Write a one- or two-paragraph response**, using the online tools (cut, copy, paste, undo, and redo) to improve your work.

PRACTICE 6

Directions: For each of the two passages, take ten minutes to read the passage and plan and write a one- or two-paragraph response to the questions in the boxes. Use multiple pieces of evidence from the text to support your response. Compose your answer on a computer if one is available or write your answer on a sheet of paper.

Short-Answer Practice: Explanation

How did the moon form? Scientists have suggested a number of answers to that question over time. Some have suggested that the moon was originally part of Earth and somehow broke off early in the history of the solar system. Others have suggested that the moon was formed separately from Earth and then at some point was drawn into Earth's gravitational field, where it remains.

Another possible answer involves rings. Earth (and other planets with a moon or moons) may have originally had rings like those of the planet Saturn. A team of scientists has recently suggested that all moons in our solar system were formed from rings. According to their idea, a moon begins to coagulate, or come together, out of debris near the outer edges of planetary rings. At those outer edges, the newly formed moon has a better chance of holding together without being broken up again by the planet's gravity. (Small objects orbiting close to a planet tend to be pulled toward the planet by gravity; they often ultimately crash into the planet.) The initial products of this process of coagulation are small "moonlets," which spin outward from the planet, colliding and fusing with other moonlets as they do so. The process is somewhat similar to that of a snowball rolling downhill, gathering more material as it rolls. This hypothesis has at least one source of appeal, in that it explains why the larger moons of planets like Neptune and Uranus (which have more than one moon) are farther away from the planet than the smaller moons.

> ### Formation of the Moon Writing Prompt
>
> Earth does not currently have rings. If Earth originally had rings, what happened to them? Using information from the passage, suggest a hypothesis to answer that question. Cite specific information from the passage as support for why your suggestion is plausible.

Short-Answer Practice: Experiment

Human blood is composed of approximately 45 percent *formed elements* (which include red blood cells, white blood cells, and platelets) and approximately 55 percent *plasma*, a liquid that holds the formed elements in suspension. The ratio of formed elements to plasma can vary according to an individual's diet, health, and genetic makeup. The ratio can be measured by taking a sample of blood and spinning it for 20 minutes in a centrifuge (a device used to separate substances) to force the formed elements to separate from the plasma. The plasma can then be siphoned off, measured, and compared to the quantity of formed elements.

Researchers are interested in learning the ways in which diet can affect the ratio of formed elements to plasma. They suspect that consumption of caffeine may have short-term effects on plasma levels relative to levels of formed elements in the blood.

> ### Caffeine and Blood Components Writing Prompt
>
> Design a controlled experiment that the researchers can use to test their hypothesis. Include descriptions of data collection and explain how the researchers would know whether their hypothesis is well supported by the experimental data.

Writing evaluation criteria begins on page 94.

SCIENCE PRACTICES PRACTICE QUESTIONS

Questions 1 through 3 are based on the following passage.

The 1543 publication of Nicolaus Copernicus's heliocentric, or sun-centered, theory of the universe marked a crucial moment in the history of science. Copernicus's theory that the planets revolve around the sun was controversial: at first, many refused to accept that Earth could be hurtling through space. However, we now know that Copernicus's theory was accurate in many ways.

Despite its importance as a breakthrough, Copernicus's theory contained a number of ideas that today seem primitive. For example, Copernicus maintained that the planets were embedded in crystalline spheres. Additionally, while Copernicus developed the novel, and later widely accepted, idea that Earth rotates on its axis, he also believed that the planets orbit around the sun in perfect circles. We now know that the planets move in elliptical orbits.

1. Which of the following is the main idea of the second paragraph?

   A. Primitive astronomers accepted Copernicus's theory when it was first published.
   B. While Copernicus's theory was an important development, it included elements that are outdated today.
   C. Copernicus believed that Earth moved around the sun, rather than the other way around.
   D. Earth does not hurtle through space.

2. Which of the following would be an appropriate title for this passage?

   A. "Important Landmarks in 16th-Century Science"
   B. "Copernicus: The Life of an Astronomer"
   C. "The Significance and Limitations of the Copernican Theory"
   D. "The Earth-Centered Universe"

3. Which of the following can be inferred from the passage?

   A. Astronomers now believe that the planets are not embedded in crystalline spheres.
   B. Astronomers now know that Earth does not move around the sun in an ellipse.
   C. All aspects of the Copernican theory have now been disproven.
   D. Copernicus took inspiration from the primitive astronomers who came before him.

4. Matter is generally found in one of three phases: solid, liquid, and gas. A substance can be converted from a solid to a liquid and then from a liquid to a gas by adding heat. Once the temperature of a solid substance reaches its melting point, any heat added is used to change the solid to the liquid phase. So, while the phase is changing, the temperature of the substance remains constant. Once the phase change is complete, the temperature of the liquid continues to rise. Similarly, once the temperature of a liquid reaches the boiling point, any heat added is used to change the liquid to the gas phase, and the temperature remains constant while the phase is changing.

Temperature and Phase Changes of a Substance

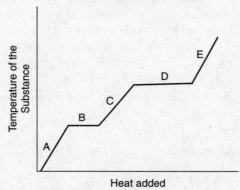

At which points are phase changes occurring in the graph above?

   A. A and E
   B. A, C, and E
   C. B and D
   D. C, D, and E

5. While all types of cancer share the common trait of uncontrolled cell growth, the causes of that uncontrolled growth are complex and varied. Nevertheless, a number of specific causes of several types of cancer are known. For example, long-term asbestos exposure can result in mesothelioma (a cancer that can affect multiple organs), while long-term regular inhalation of tobacco smoke can lead to lung cancer. In addition to such chemical causes, viruses are also responsible for a number of types of cancer: human papillomavirus precipitates cervical cancer, while the hepatitis B virus causes liver cancer.

Use the information above to place four specific types of cancer from the list below into the left side of the table. Place a corresponding cause of each, as identified in the passage above, into the cell immediately to its right.

Type of Cancer	Cause

hepatitis B	mesothelioma
human papillomavirus	cervical cancer
long-term asbestos exposure	liver cancer
lung cancer	long-term inhalation of tobacco smoke

Questions 6 through 8 are based on the following paragraph and graphic.

Record high temperatures were recorded in numerous Australian cities in the summer of 2012. The chart below indicates current and former record temperatures for seven of those cities. For instance, Hobart's previous record was a little below 41°C, and its current record is a little above 41°C.

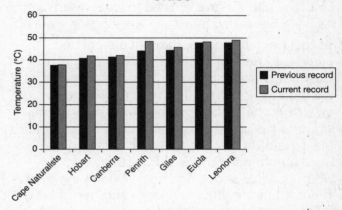

Record High Temperatures in Australian Cities

6. According to the chart, which city experienced the largest increase from its previous record to its current record?

   A. Hobart
   B. Penrith
   C. Eucla
   D. Leonora

7. Which of the following cities had a previous record equal to the median of all the cities' previous records?

   A. Cape Naturaliste
   B. Canberra
   C. Penrith
   D. Eucla

8. According to the chart, which of the following statements is true?

   A. Temperatures will likely continue to increase.
   B. Temperatures increased 5 degrees or less.
   C. Temperatures increased more than 5 degrees.
   D. Temperatures usually increase 2–5 degrees in the summer.

Questions 9 through 12 are based on the following passage.

An office manager noticed that each time she touched the metal filing cabinet next to her desk, she experienced an electrostatic shock (commonly known as "static"). Her assistant, however, only rarely experienced such shocks when touching the cabinet. The office manager wondered why this might be.

The office manager developed a hypothesis: perhaps differences in clothing could explain why she was experiencing more shocks than her assistant. The office manager liked to wear nylon clothing, and her assistant usually wore cotton clothing.

To test her hypothesis, the office manager convinced her assistant to wear nylon clothing to work every day for a week, while she herself wore cotton clothing. The next week, they switched: the office manager wore nylon clothing, and the assistant wore cotton. To control for the possibility that the differences in shocks were due to differences in their footwear, they wore identical shoes each day. During the experiment, both the office manager and her assistant recorded the number of times they touched the metal filing cabinet each day, and they also recorded the number of times they experienced electrostatic shocks when doing so.

At the end of the first week, they found that the assistant had experienced 73 electrostatic shocks, while the office manager had experienced 10. During the second week, the office manager experienced 68 shocks, and her assistant 12. The office manager concluded that these results supported her hypothesis, and as a result she decided to switch to wearing mostly cotton clothing.

9. Scientific investigations begin with a question. Which of the following is the question that formed the basis for the office manager's experiment?

   A. Is it better to wear cotton clothing or nylon clothing?
   B. Why does touching the metal filing cabinet produce more electrostatic shocks than touching other office furniture?
   C. Why, when I touch the metal filing cabinet, do I experience more electrostatic shocks than my assistant does when she touches it?
   D. Could my shoes be causing me to experience more electrostatic shocks than my assistant experiences?

10. Which of the following best summarizes how the office manager conducted her experiment?

   A. The office manager suspected that her nylon clothing was causing her to experience electrostatic shocks.
   B. The office manager switched to cotton clothing after seeing that her hypothesis was supported by her data.
   C. The office manager wore shoes of a different material than those of her assistant.
   D. The office manager wore one type of clothing, while her assistant wore another type of clothing, and they recorded the number of shocks they experienced.

11. Why did the office manager and her assistant wear the same type of shoes while conducting the experiment?

   A. They wanted to test the effect of their clothing on the number of shocks they experienced, and wearing different types of shoes might have confused their results.
   B. They wanted to test whether the office manager's shoes were causing the high number of electrostatic shocks she was experiencing.
   C. They believed that wearing cotton might cause the wearer to experience more electrostatic shocks.
   D. They wanted to protect themselves from the effects of electrostatic shock.

12. Imagine that the results of the office manager's experiment had demonstrated that her clothing was not in fact responsible for the large number of electrostatic shocks she was experiencing. After reviewing those findings, the office manager then wondered if her footwear might be responsible, and she decided to conduct a new experiment to test this idea. Before she conducted that experiment, the idea that her shoes might be responsible would be which of the following?

   A. a new conclusion based on findings
   B. a general principle from the study of physics
   C. a new hypothesis
   D. an experiment design

Directions: You MAY use your calculator to figure out the answers to questions 13 and 14.

13. Common garden snails are hermaphroditic. That is, each individual snail produces both sperm and eggs. Mating between two garden snails involves the transfer of sperm from each partner to the other. A high school science teacher has created a large terrarium for his classroom that contains 6 adult garden snails. Assuming that all 6 snails are healthy, how many different mating pairs are possible?

    A. 2
    B. 12
    C. 15
    D. 36

14. The sun is a class G star, which is a type of main-sequence star. Approximately 90 percent of all stars in the Milky Way galaxy are main-sequence stars, and approximately 7 percent of all main-sequence stars are class G stars. What is the probability that any given star in the Milky Way galaxy is a class G star? Express your answer as a percentage:

Directions: Use ten minutes to read, plan, and write a one- or two-paragraph response to this short-answer activity. Compose your answer on a computer if one is available or write your answer on a separate sheet of paper.

15. The table below contains data observed in a group of 58-year-old Swedish men. The study examined the relationship between tobacco use and formations called plaques that build up on the walls of arteries, which are blood vessels that carry blood from the heart to the body's tissues. The carotid and femoral arteries are two large and very important arteries.

Average Characteristics of 58-Year-Old Swedish Men, by Smoking Status

	Never Smokers	Ex-Smokers	Current Smokers
Waist circumference (cm)	93.8	99.1	95.4
Cholesterol			
Total Cholesterol	5.98	6.11	5.90
HDL Cholesterol	1.31	1.28	1.21
LDL Cholesterol	4.08	4.09	3.95
Carotid plaques (%)			
None	62	55	53
Small	15	23	16
Large	23	22	31
Femoral plaques (%)			
None	80	54	45
Small	10	13	14
Large	10	33	41

Swedish Men and Smoking Writing Prompt

Discuss the conclusions that can be drawn from the information recorded in the table above, making specific reference to the data. In addition, identify any further information that would need to be obtained in order to better evaluate the relationship between plaque formation and smoking.

Answers and explanations start on page 94.

LIFE SCIENCE

Cell Structures and Functions

Key Ideas

- The basic unit of all living things is the cell, which carries out the life functions, including movement, growth, and reproduction.
- All cells have a cell membrane, cytoplasm, and genetic material.
- Unlike an animal cell, a plant cell contains a cell wall—a structure that gives the cell rigidity and shape.

GED® TEST TIP

The title and labels of a diagram usually tell you the main idea of the diagram. Here, the main idea is that plant cells have cell structures with specialized functions.

All living things are made of **cells**, the basic unit of life. Some organisms, like bacteria and protozoa, are **unicellular**—they consist of a single cell. Others, like plants and animals, are **multicellular**, consisting of many different types of specialized cells. For example, humans have skin cells, blood cells, and nerve cells, to name just a few. All cells carry out the basic life functions: movement, growth, cell maintenance, reproduction, and the manufacture of specialized substances.

Although cells differ widely in size and appearance, they all have basic structures in common. All cells have a **cell membrane**, a structure that keeps the cell's contents separate from its external environment. The cell membrane is selectively permeable, which means that it allows certain substances, such as water, nutrients, and wastes, to pass between the cell's interior and the surrounding environment. Inside the cell membrane is the **cytoplasm**, a watery, jellylike substance that can include other cell structures. Finally, all cells have **genetic material**, which contains coded instructions for carrying out the cell's activities. In bacteria, the genetic material consists of a single molecule suspended in the cytoplasm. Bacteria are called **prokaryotes**. In all other cells, the genetic material is contained within a **nucleus**. Such cells are called **eukaryotic cells**. All plant and animal cells are eukaryotic. A typical plant cell is shown below. Note that a plant cell has a **cell wall**, which gives the cell shape and rigidity, and an animal cell does not.

A Plant Cell

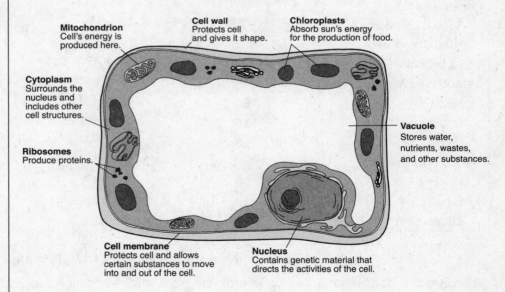

Mitochondrion
Cell's energy is produced here.

Cell wall
Protects cell and gives it shape.

Chloroplasts
Absorb sun's energy for the production of food.

Cytoplasm
Surrounds the nucleus and includes other cell structures.

Vacuole
Stores water, nutrients, wastes, and other substances.

Ribosomes
Produce proteins.

Cell membrane
Protects cell and allows certain substances to move into and out of the cell.

Nucleus
Contains genetic material that directs the activities of the cell.

PRACTICE 1

<u>Questions 1 through 3</u> are based on the information on page 42.

1. According to the diagram on page 42, the function of the [Select... ▾] is to supply energy to the cell.

   - nucleus
   - ribosomes
   - mitochondrion

2. In addition to the cell wall, the water stored in a plant cell's vacuole helps give the plant firmness and shape. When a plant is not taking in enough water from the soil through its roots, it uses up its stored water and its vacuoles shrink. When the vacuoles shrink, the plant wilts.

   Which of the following is a conclusion based on the paragraph above rather than a given fact?

   A. Cell walls help give a plant cell firmness and shape.
   B. Vacuoles help give a plant cell firmness and shape.
   C. Plants take in water from the soil through their roots.
   D. Cell walls cannot maintain a plant's shape and rigidity when the plant lacks water.

3. A student is examining a cell using a microscope. She is able to identify the cell membrane, cytoplasm, a small vacuole, and the nucleus, but she does not see a cell wall or any chloroplasts. She concludes that the cell is a eukaryotic cell.

   Which of the following is evidence that her conclusion is correct?

   A. the presence of a nucleus
   B. the presence of cytoplasm
   C. the absence of chloroplasts
   D. the absence of a cell wall

4. Cells were first seen during the 1600s, when English scientist Robert Hooke observed cork cell walls through a microscope that could magnify a specimen a couple of hundred times its original size. In the 1800s, the compound light microscope, which magnifies up to a thousand times, was developed. Electron microscopes, which can magnify up to a million times, were invented during the 1900s.

   Which of the following best explains why our knowledge of cells has grown with improvements in microscope technology?

   A. Each time the microscope is improved, scientists can see cell structures more clearly.
   B. With the first microscopes, all cell structures were clearly visible.
   C. Compound light microscopes can magnify cells up to a thousand times.
   D. Robert Hooke's microscope only allowed him to see the largest cell structures.

5. Diffusion is a process by which particles move from an area of higher concentration to an area of lower concentration. For example, oxygen diffuses through the cell membrane of a unicellular pond organism from the water, where there is lots of oxygen, into the cell, where there is less oxygen. Eventually, the concentration of oxygen inside and outside the unicellular organism is the same.

   What would happen if the concentration of oxygen were greater in the unicellular organism than in its watery environment?

   A. Water would diffuse from the unicellular organism into the pond water.
   B. Oxygen would diffuse from the unicellular organism into the pond water.
   C. Oxygen would diffuse from the pond water into the unicellular organism.
   D. Diffusion of oxygen between the organism and the pond water would stop entirely.

Answers and explanations start on page 95.

LIFE SCIENCE

Cell Processes and Energy

Key Ideas

- In photosynthesis, plants use light energy to form glucose from carbon dioxide and water. Oxygen is a by-product.
- In cellular respiration, glucose is broken down in the presence of oxygen to release energy. Carbon dioxide is a by-product.
- These two processes help maintain oxygen and carbon dioxide levels in the atmosphere.

ON THE GED® TEST

About 40% of the questions on the Science Test *are about life science topics.*

All cells need energy to carry out the life functions, such as growth and reproduction. Green plants, some algae, and some bacteria use energy from sunlight to make food in a process called **photosynthesis**.

In photosynthesis, plants use sunlight to power chemical reactions that convert carbon dioxide gas and water into oxygen and the simple sugar **glucose**. In the first stage of photosynthesis, light energy is captured by chloroplasts inside plant cells. Chloroplasts contain **chlorophyll**, a pigment that gives plants their green color. Chlorophyll absorbs light energy for photosynthesis. In the second stage, water (H_2O) that the plant gets from the soil and carbon dioxide (CO_2) that the plant gets from the air undergo a complex series of chemical reactions inside the chloroplasts. The products of these reactions are oxygen (O_2) and glucose $(C_6H_{12}O_6)$. Plant cells use the energy that is stored in glucose to power cell processes. Photosynthesis can be summarized in the chemical equation shown below:

$$light\ energy$$
$$6CO_2 + 6H_2O \rightarrow C_6H_{12}O_6 + 6O_2$$

In words, this means that carbon dioxide plus water, in the presence of light energy, yields glucose plus oxygen.

As a result of photosynthesis, energy is stored in sugars and other **carbohydrates** in the plant. To meet their energy needs, other organisms eat plants or eat organisms that eat plants. When energy is needed in a cell, carbohydrates are broken down to release the energy in a process called **cellular respiration**. In this process, oxygen from the air reacts with glucose from food to yield carbon dioxide, water, and energy. Cellular respiration can be summarized in the following chemical equation:

$$C_6H_{12}O_6 + 6O_2 \rightarrow 6CO_2 + 6H_2O + energy$$

In words, this means that glucose plus oxygen yields carbon dioxide, water, and energy.

If you examine the two equations, you will notice that the products of photosynthesis are the raw materials of cellular respiration, and the products of cellular respiration are the raw materials of photosynthesis. These two processes are part of a cycle. Plants release oxygen, a waste product of photosynthesis, into the atmosphere. Animals breathe in the oxygen and use it in cellular respiration. They breathe out carbon dioxide, a waste product of cellular respiration. The carbon dioxide is then used by plants in photosynthesis, and the cycle repeats. Between them, photosynthesis and cellular respiration help keep the amounts of oxygen and carbon dioxide in the atmosphere fairly constant.

PRACTICE 2

<u>Questions 1 through 3</u> are based on the information on page 44.

1. Which of the following are the products of cellular respiration?

   A. glucose and light energy
   B. carbon dioxide and oxygen
   C. glucose, oxygen, and energy
   D. carbon dioxide, water, and energy

2. A horticulturist wants to grow large, healthy plants by maximizing the rate of photosynthesis.

   Which of the following actions would be most likely to get the results she wants?

   A. increasing the amount of light the plants receive each day
   B. increasing the amount of oxygen the plants receive each day
   C. decreasing the amount of oxygen the plants receive each day
   D. decreasing the amount of carbon dioxide the plants receive each day

3. Carbon dioxide is one of the "greenhouse gases" that help keep Earth warm by trapping radiated heat in the atmosphere. Global warming is thought to be caused in part by increased amounts of carbon dioxide in the atmosphere.

   Which of the following would help reduce the level of carbon dioxide in the atmosphere and thus perhaps slow the global warming trend?

   A. increasing the population of domestic animals
   B. increasing the number of green plants
   C. increasing the harvest of trees
   D. increasing the amount of glucose in our food

<u>Questions 4 and 5</u> refer to the following information and diagram.

In most plants, photosynthesis takes place primarily in the palisade cells of leaves.

Cross Section of a Leaf

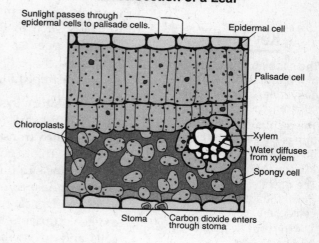

4. <u>Fill in the blank</u> using one word from the diagram.

   A(n) _____ is an opening in the lower surface of the leaf through which gases such as carbon dioxide can pass.

5. Chloroplasts are structures found within some of the cells in a leaf. They help in the process of photosynthesis. In the diagram, they are represented by small gray spots on the cells.

   Which of the following statements is supported by the information in the diagram?

   A. Palisade cells provide a means of transporting water through a plant.
   B. Most of a leaf's chloroplasts are found in its palisade cells.
   C. The spongy cells are soft, like a sponge.
   D. The epidermis blocks light from reaching the palisade cells.

Answers and explanations start on page 96.

LIFE SCIENCE

Human Body Systems

- The circulatory system moves blood around the body, delivering and taking away substances.
- The respiratory system brings oxygen into the body and gets rid of carbon dioxide.
- The digestive system breaks down food into nutrients that cells can use.
- The nervous system controls body activities.

ON THE GED® TEST

On the Science Test, you will have to answer questions that require you to use information from both text and a graphic, as in questions 4 and 5 on page 47.

There are four levels of organization in the human body: (1) **cells**, the smallest unit of life; (2) **tissues**, groups of similar cells that perform a specific function, such as muscle tissue; (3) **organs**, groups of tissues that perform a function, such as the stomach; and (4) **body systems**, groups of organs working together to perform a function, such as digestion. Human body systems include the circulatory, respiratory, digestive, nervous, immune, endocrine, reproductive, urinary, skeletal, and muscular systems.

The **circulatory system**, sometimes called the cardiovascular system, consists of the heart and the blood vessels. Its main function is to move the blood, which transports substances like oxygen and nutrients, throughout the body. The major **organ** of the circulatory system is the **heart**, a muscle that contracts to pump blood. Blood moves through the blood vessels from large **arteries**, to smaller arteries, to **capillaries**, to small **veins**, to large veins, and back to the heart. Through the thin walls of the capillaries, oxygen, nutrients, and other substances pass from the blood into the body's cells, and carbon dioxide and other wastes pass from the cells into the blood.

The **respiratory system** consists of the nose, throat, **trachea** (windpipe), and **lungs**. Its function is to take oxygen from the air into the body when we inhale and to get rid of waste in the form of carbon dioxide when we exhale. The trachea branches into two tubes called the **bronchi**, one of which goes into each lung. The bronchi branch into smaller tubes called **bronchioles**, each of which ends in an **alveolus**, a tiny spherical sac. Inside the capillaries of the alveoli, oxygen diffuses into the blood and carbon dioxide diffuses out of the blood.

The **digestive system** consists of the mouth, **esophagus**, **stomach**, **small intestine**, and **large intestine**. Its function is to break down food into nutrients, which are used for cell processes including the production of energy, and to get rid of digestive wastes. Digestion begins in the mouth, where the teeth grind food into smaller pieces, and **saliva** begins to break it down chemically. Food is pushed by muscular action down through the esophagus into the stomach, where it is churned and further broken down by **enzymes** and stomach acids. From the stomach it travels to the small intestine, where most of the nutrients are absorbed into the blood through tiny capillaries in the **villi**. What remains goes to the large intestine, which removes water, leaving solid waste to be excreted through the **rectum**.

The **nervous system** consists of the **brain**, **spinal cord**, and **nerves**. Its function is to receive, process, and transmit information, controlling body activities. The brain has three main parts: the **cerebrum**, which controls functions such as thinking, seeing, and speaking; the **cerebellum**, which coordinates movement and position; and the **brainstem**, which controls breathing and heart rate. Information is transmitted to and from the brain through the nerves, which are bundled in the spinal cord and branch out from there into all parts of the body.

PRACTICE 3

Questions 1 through 3 are based on the information on page 46.

1. Which human body system interacts with each cell of the body?

   A. the circulatory system
   B. the digestive system
   C. the muscular system
   D. the skeletal system

2. How are the alveoli in the lungs and the villi in the small intestine similar?

   A. Both are structures located in the respiratory system.
   B. Both are structures located in the digestive system.
   C. Both are structures in which substances pass through capillary walls into the blood.
   D. Both are structures involved in coordination and movement.

3. In the 17th century, English physician William Harvey concluded that blood in the veins flows toward the heart.

   Which of the following facts helps support Harvey's conclusion?

   A. The heart pumps about 1,800 gallons of blood per day.
   B. The heart has four chambers: two atria and two ventricles.
   C. Large veins branch into smaller blood vessels called capillaries.
   D. Veins have valves that allow blood to flow in one direction only.

Questions 4 and 5 refer to the following information and diagram.

The kidneys of the urinary system remove cellular wastes and excess water from the blood. This material, called urine, is stored in the bladder until it is excreted from the body.

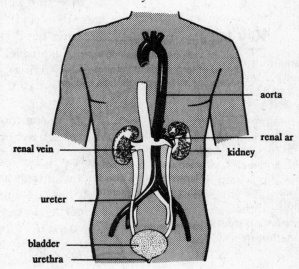

4. On the diagram, circle the name(s) of the structure(s) through which urine passes from the kidneys to the bladder.

5. A urologist is a doctor who specializes in disorders of the urinary system.

   Which of the following patients is most likely to be treated by a urologist?

   A. a patient with low levels of iron in her blood
   B. a patient with a painful kidney stone
   C. a patient with swollen veins in the anus, called hemorrhoids
   D. a patient with chronic indigestion

Answers and explanations start on page 96.

LIFE SCIENCE

Health Issues

Health can be affected by infections, nutrition, and substance abuse.

An **infection** is the invasion of the body by germs—microorganisms that cause disease. It is often characterized by fever and other symptoms. Germs can enter the body through breaks in the skin (for example, tetanus), with air (for example, influenza), in contaminated food and water (for example, food poisoning), by contact with contaminated blood or saliva (for example, rabies), or through sexual activity (for example, gonorrhea). Infections can be grouped according to the type of microorganisms that cause them. The most common germs are **bacteria** and **viruses**, although infections can also be caused by fungi, protozoans, and worms.

The body has natural defenses against infection, such as the skin, the mucous membranes in the nose, tears, and acid in the stomach. If germs get past these defenses, the **immune system** produces **antibodies** that destroy the germs. In developed nations, infectious diseases are less common than they used to be because of better nutrition and living conditions, safer water and sewage systems, **immunization** (which provides protection against specific infectious diseases), and **antibiotics**, drugs that fight bacteria.

Nutrients are substances that are needed for growth, normal functioning, and maintenance of cells. The body does not produce nutrients; instead we get them from the food we eat. The nutrients that humans need for good health include **proteins**, **carbohydrates** (sugars and starches), **fats**, **vitamins**, **minerals**, and water. In a well-balanced diet, people get enough nutrients to provide energy as well as the right nutrients needed for all the body's functions. Too much or too little of a nutrient can cause problems. For example, a diet with too much fat can lead to obesity and contribute to heart disease. Too little vitamin C can cause scurvy, a painful disease.

Drugs are substances that affect the structure or function of the body. They are usually used to treat disease or relieve its symptoms, although some drugs, like nicotine in tobacco, have no medicinal purpose. The nonmedical use of a drug to the point that it interferes with a person's normal functioning is called **drug abuse**, or substance abuse. Drug abuse can lead to **addiction**, a severe form of dependence that causes physical changes in the body so that when the drug wears off or is stopped, withdrawal symptoms such as nausea and pain occur. Heroin, speed, alcohol, nicotine, and barbiturates are frequently abused addictive drugs. A milder form of dependence than addiction is **psychological dependence**, or **habituation**. In this type of dependence, the urge to take the drug is strong, even though there are no withdrawal symptoms. Examples of drugs that can cause habituation in humans are marijuana and hallucinogens. People also abuse substances that are not drugs, like glue, gasoline, and aerosols. Most of these substances are **inhalants**—they are sniffed for their effect on the nervous system. Inhalants generally depress, or slow, the functioning of the nervous system, sometimes causing their users to lose control or become unconscious.

Key Ideas

- Infections occur when the body is invaded by germs—microorganisms that cause disease.
- A healthy diet has the right nutrients—proteins, carbohydrates, fats, vitamins, minerals, and water.
- The abuse of drugs and other substances can cause physical changes and interfere with a person's daily functioning.

ON THE GED® TEST

Many of the questions on the GED® Science Test are in multiple-choice format. For each question, you must pick the one correct answer from the four options that are given.

PRACTICE 4

Questions 1 and 2 are based on the information on page 48.

1. Which of the following is among the body's first barriers against germs?

   A. the immune system
   B. antibiotics
   C. antibodies
   D. the skin

2. Each evening, Sara has a glass of wine. If there is no wine in the house, she feels a strong urge to get some, although she feels no ill effects if she does not.

   What is Sara's relationship to alcohol?

   A. addiction
   B. physical dependence
   C. habituation
   D. withdrawal

Questions 3 and 4 are based on the following table.

Nutrients in the Diet

Nutrient	Description	Function	Source
Proteins	Complex molecules (amino acids) made of oxygen, carbon, nitrogen, hydrogen	Growth and maintenance of cells and metabolism	Meat, fish, eggs, dairy products, legumes, nuts, seeds
Carbohydrates	Molecules containing oxygen, carbon, and hydrogen	Body's main energy source, providing 4 calories of energy per gram; roughage for digestion	Bread, pasta, cereal, rice, fruits, potatoes
Fats	Fatty acids containing oxygen, carbon, and hydrogen	Concentrated source of energy, providing 9 calories of energy per gram; insulation; cell maintenance	Fish oils, vegetable oils, and animal fats
Vitamins	Substances used in very small quantities that are vital for body chemistry	Growth maintenance, repair of cells; protein synthesis; metabolism; and other functions	Various foods, daylight on skin (vitamin D), microorganisms in the bowel (vitamin K)
Minerals	Substances, such as iron and calcium, necessary for normal development	Many functions, including making red blood cells and building strong bones	Various foods
Water	A liquid made of oxygen and hydrogen atoms	Involved in almost all body processes	Beverages, soups, foods

3. Which of the following statements is supported by the information in the table?

   A. Fats are a more concentrated source of energy than carbohydrates.
   B. Vitamins are more important in the diet than minerals.
   C. A good source of vitamin C is citrus fruits.
   D. Minerals provide a low-fat source of energy.

4. Which of the following is a fact, rather than an opinion, based on the table?

   A. Eating meat is the best way to get sufficient protein in your diet.
   B. Carbohydrates come from fruits as well as from bread and rice.
   C. Iron is the only mineral you need.
   D. Everyone should drink eight glasses of water each day.

Answers and explanations start on page 96.

LIFE SCIENCE

Reproduction and Heredity

Key Ideas

- In asexual reproduction, an offspring is identical to its parent; in sexual reproduction, an offspring is unique, inheriting traits from each parent.
- Gregor Mendel was the first to observe patterns of trait inheritance.
- Traits are controlled by genes, which come in forms called alleles. A dominant allele hides a recessive allele.

GED® TEST TIP

As you take the test, pace yourself. If you are unsure of an answer, do your best and mark Flag for Review at the top of your computer screen. At the end of the test, you may have time to review these "flagged" questions.

All **species** of organisms reproduce in some way. There are two types of reproduction. In **asexual reproduction**, an individual organism produces offspring identical to the parent. For example, in a type of asexual reproduction called budding, a tiny freshwater animal called a hydra grows buds that develop into offspring. In **sexual reproduction**, two sex cells combine to form unique offspring with characteristics from both parent cells. In humans and many other species, those specialized sex cells are called **sperm** and **ova**.

Physical characteristics of organisms are called **traits**. The passing of traits from parents to offspring in sexual reproduction is called **heredity**. The first person to study heredity in a systematic way was an Austrian monk, **Gregor Mendel** (1822–1884). He bred plants and observed that sometimes offspring plants had the same traits as the parents and sometimes they did not. Mendel experimented with **purebred** pea plants—plants that always produced offspring with the same form of a trait as the parent. For example, purebred short plants always produced short offspring. First he crossed purebred short plants with purebred tall plants. In the first generation of offspring, all the plants were tall—the shortness trait had vanished. When the first-generation offspring reproduced, about three-quarters of the next generation of plants were tall, and one-quarter were short. The shortness trait had reappeared.

Mendel repeated his pea plant experiments with other traits over a ten-year period. Eventually he concluded that individual factors from each parent plant control the **inheritance** of specific traits. An offspring plant inherited one factor from the female parent and one from the male parent. Mendel concluded that one factor in a pair can hide the other factor. For example, the tallness factor hid the shortness factor in the first generation of offspring.

The factors that control traits are called **genes**. Different forms of a gene are called **alleles**. The gene that controls pea plant height, for example, has one allele for tallness and one allele for shortness. Each pea plant inherits one allele for the height gene from each parent. Therefore, any particular pea plant may have (1) two alleles for tallness, (2) two alleles for shortness, or (3) one allele for shortness and one for tallness. In the third case, the **dominant allele**, the tallness allele, controls the appearance of the trait. The **recessive allele**, the shortness allele, is hidden. For a recessive trait to appear in an individual, the individual must inherit two recessive alleles.

In Mendel's original experiment, the parent plants were purebred tall and purebred short. Thus, one parent had two dominant alleles for tallness, and the other parent had two recessive alleles for shortness. All the offspring in the first generation were **hybrid**—each had one allele for tallness and one for shortness. Because the tallness allele is dominant, all of the first generation plants were tall. In the next generation, some plants inherited two dominant alleles, some inherited two recessive alleles, and some inherited one dominant and one recessive allele, producing a mix of plants.

PRACTICE 5

Questions 1 through 3 refer to the following paragraph and diagram.

The Punnett square below shows all the possible combinations of alleles for height in offspring pea plants when two tall hybrid pea plants are crossed. A capital *T* represents the dominant tallness allele, and a lowercase *t*, the recessive shortness allele. One parent's alleles are shown along the top of the square; the other's are shown on the left side. The **genotypes** of the offspring are shown in the boxes.

	T	t
T	T T	T t
t	T t	t t

1. The parent pea plants are both [Select... ⌄] .

   - tall
   - short
   - of medium height

2. What chance is there that an offspring will be short?

   A. 0 out of 4
   B. 1 out of 4
   C. 2 out of 4
   D. 3 out of 4

3. If you wanted to grow only tall pea plants in your garden over several growing seasons, which of the following genotypes would give you the best results?

   A. tt
   B. Tt
   C. tT
   D. TT

4. Fill in the blank with a numeral.

   According to the passage on page 50, in order to show a recessive trait, an organism must inherit _____ recessive alleles for that trait.

5. Why are organisms that reproduce sexually more genetically diverse than organisms that reproduce asexually?

   A. Organisms that reproduce sexually tend to produce more offspring than those that reproduce asexually.
   B. Organisms that reproduce sexually produce offspring that inherit diverse traits from only one parent.
   C. Organisms that reproduce sexually produce offspring with entirely new traits unlike those of either parent.
   D. Organisms that reproduce sexually produce offspring that have inherited a mix of traits from their parents.

6. A student is trying to repeat Mendel's experiments using the trait of fur color in rabbits. Black fur is dominant, and white fur is recessive. She starts with what she assumes is a purebred white female rabbit and a purebred black male rabbit. She crosses them and is surprised when one of the offspring has white fur.

   What probably was wrong with the student's experiment?

   A. The white female was actually a hybrid.
   B. The black male was actually a hybrid.
   C. Most of the offspring were hybrids.
   D. Most of the offspring were purebred.

   Answers and explanations start on page 96.

Modern Genetics

Key Ideas

- Chromosomes are structures in a cell's nucleus that are composed mostly of genes, which are located on long molecules of DNA.
- DNA contains the genetic code for making proteins in the cell.
- Knowledge of genetics has led to advances in many fields but especially in medicine.

Years after Mendel died, scientists identified **chromosomes**, rod-shaped structures in the nucleus of each cell, as responsible for carrying genes from parent organisms to their offspring. Reproductive cells have half the number of chromosomes of an organism's other cells. When a sperm cell and an ovum unite, the resulting offspring has a full set of chromosomes. For example, human sex cells have 23 chromosomes and our other cells have 46.

One chromosome can contain thousands of genes on a single long molecule of **deoxyribonucleic acid (DNA)**. A DNA molecule is shaped like a spiral ladder. The sides of the ladder are made of deoxyribose—a sugar— and phosphate. Each rung of the ladder is made of a pair of nitrogen bases. There are four of these bases: adenine (A), guanine (G), thymine (T), and cytosine (C). The four bases pair up in a specific way: *A* always pairs with *T*, and *C* always pairs with *G*.

DNA

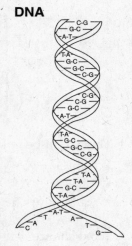

DNA controls the cell's production of proteins, which help determine all the characteristics and processes of the organism. During **protein synthesis**, the information from a gene in the cell's nucleus is used to produce a protein on ribosomes in the cytoplasm. Messenger **ribonucleic acid (RNA)**, transmits the code from the DNA. Each set of three base pairs on the messenger RNA, called a **codon**, contains instructions for creating an **amino acid**—a protein building block. The sequence of codons determines the sequence of amino acids in the protein and thus the specific protein to be made. So, the order of bases on the gene forms a **genetic code** for the synthesis of a particular protein.

ON THE GED® TEST

Some questions on the GED® Test are based entirely on a graphic. Read the title of the diagram, chart, or graph to make sure you understand its main idea before you answer questions based on it.

There have been many recent advances in genetics, some controversial. Dolly the sheep and other animals have been cloned from single cells. Cloning bypasses sexual reproduction, raising the possibility that one day humans will be cloned—an idea that many find unethical. Through genetic engineering, the DNA of one organism can be introduced into the DNA of another organism, changing the second organism's traits. Genetic engineering has been used to produce medicines, such as insulin. It has been more controversial when used to improve foods. Finally, the entire **human genome**, or genetic code, has been decoded, making possible many advances in medicine. Scientists have identified genes involved in genetic disorders such as cystic fibrosis. They have also identified genes that predispose people to diseases such as breast cancer and Alzheimer's disease. Through genetic testing, people can find out whether they have any of these disease-related genes. In some cases, they can take steps to prevent the disease or to seek early treatment. In recent years, scientists have also succeeded in correcting certain genetic disorders through gene therapy.

PRACTICE 6

Questions 1 and 2 are based on the information on page 52.

1. Which of the following provides the code needed for a cell to make proteins?

   A. the number of chromosomes in the cell
   B. the amino acids in the cytoplasm
   C. the sequence of base pairs in a gene
   D. the pairing of adenine with thymine

2. A mutation is any change in the DNA of a gene. Which of the following is the most likely result of a mutation?

   A. the loss of one or more chromosomes
   B. an extra chromosome
   C. too much RNA in the cytoplasm
   D. a change in protein synthesis

---

3. Some animals have been genetically engineered to grow larger. Plants have been engineered to resist diseases or insects. Some fruits have been engineered to ripen more slowly. Genetic engineering of domesticated plants and animals is controversial. According to some people, these foods pose a risk because their effects on consumers and the environment are unknown. Others claim that genetically engineered foods are safe.

   Which of the following statements is an opinion about genetic engineering rather than a fact?

   A. Scientists have used genetic engineering to produce animals that grow larger.
   B. Disease-resistant plants have been produced by genetic engineering.
   C. Some genetically engineered fruit takes longer to ripen than its unaltered counterpart.
   D. Genetically engineered foods are safe for consumers and the environment.

4. When a cell reproduces through cell division, scientists call the reproducing cell the parent cell, and the two cells that result from the division are called daughter cells. The daughter cells are genetically identical to the parent cells. Before a parent cell starts to divide, the DNA in its nucleus replicates, or makes a complete copy of itself.

   Why is this process necessary?

   A. so that the parent cell will have an extra copy of DNA
   B. so that each daughter cell receives a complete set of DNA
   C. so that each daughter cell will not need to synthesize proteins
   D. so that each daughter cell will receive half its DNA from each parent cell

5. Which of the following statements is supported by the diagram and the passage on page 52?

   A. The DNA molecule unzips between the sugar and phosphate segments.
   B. The base guanine pairs only with the base cytosine.
   C. In a sequence of DNA bases, guanine always comes before adenine.
   D. About 10 percent of DNA contains genes; the remainder is "junk" DNA.

6. According to the passage on page 52, proteins, which perform a variety of functions, are built from chains of Select... ▾ .

   • amino acids
   • RNA
   • codons
   • enzymes

Answers and explanations start on page 97.

LIFE SCIENCE

Evolution and Natural Selection

Key Ideas

- Charles Darwin's observations in the Galápagos Islands led him to formulate the theory of evolution.
- Adaptations are traits that help an organism survive in its environment.
- Natural selection is the process by which individuals with favorable variations survive, reproduce, and pass the variations to their offspring.

ON THE GED® TEST

The GED® Science Test will not test memorized definitions of terms such as "adaptation" and "natural selection." However, you could be asked a question about the meaning of a term in the context of a science passage.

In 1831, the British ship the *Beagle* set sail with naturalist Charles Darwin (1809–1882) aboard. Darwin's job was to observe living things he encountered. His observations during this five-year trip around the world led him to formulate an important scientific theory, the theory of **evolution**.

One of the *Beagle*'s stops was the Galápagos Islands, a group of islands in the Pacific Ocean off the South American coast. There Darwin saw great diversity of life forms. He noticed that many of the plants and animals resembled those he had seen on the South American mainland. However, there were also important differences between mainland and island organisms. For example, the iguanas on the mainland had small claws that allowed them to climb trees to eat leaves. On the Galápagos, iguanas had large claws that allowed them to grip wet, slippery rocks and eat seaweed. As Darwin traveled among the Galápagos Islands, he also observed that similar species of organisms sometimes differed from island to island. For example, small birds called ground finches had strong, wide beaks well-suited for breaking and eating seeds. However, different species of ground finches had different sized beaks, depending on which island they lived on. The sizes of the iguanas' claws and the birds' beaks are examples of **adaptations**, traits that help an organism survive in its environment. From these observations, Darwin concluded that organisms had originally come from the mainland and had changed, or evolved, over many generations to become better adapted to their new island environments.

Darwin explained that species evolve because of **natural selection**. By this process, individuals that are better adapted to their environments are more likely to survive and reproduce, passing their favorable adaptations to their offspring. Several factors are involved in natural selection:

1. Most species produce far more offspring than can survive.
2. These offspring compete with one another for scarce resources in their environment.
3. Members of a species have different traits, called **variations**. Some variations make individuals better adapted to survive in their environment.
4. Individuals with favorable variations are more likely to survive, reproduce, and pass the favorable traits to their offspring.
5. Over generations, helpful variations spread through a species, causing the species to change, or evolve.

Evolution through natural selection explains how species change over time. But how do new species evolve? Geographic isolation seems to play a big role in the evolution of new species. When a group of individuals remains separated from the rest of its species long enough, it may become a new species. This means that members of the new species will be unable to interbreed with members of the original species. For example, there are 13 species of finches on the various Galápagos Islands. They all probably evolved from a single ancestral species.

PRACTICE 7

Questions 1 and 2 refer to the following paragraph and diagram.

The forelimbs of humans, penguins, birds that fly, and alligators are similar. The similar pattern of the bones is evidence that these animals evolved from a common ancestor. Similar structures that organisms have inherited from a common ancestor are called homologous structures.

Homologous Structures

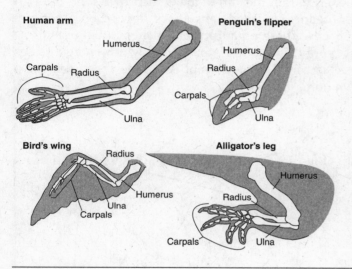

1. The forelimbs of frogs are homologous to those of human arms, penguins' flippers, birds' wings, and alligators' legs. Based on the diagram and paragraph, which of the following is likely to be true of frogs' forelimbs?

    A. Frogs use their forelimbs for swimming.
    B. Frogs' forelimbs contain carpal bones.
    C. Frogs' forelimbs resemble wings more than they resemble human arms.
    D. Frogs are more closely related to humans than they are to alligators.

2. Which of the following statements is supported by the paragraph and the diagram?

    A. The tip of a bird's wing is homologous to the upper arm of a human.
    B. Penguins are more closely related to humans than they are to birds.
    C. In penguins, flying birds, humans, and alligators, the forelimbs have similar structures despite performing different functions.
    D. Homologous structures have similar functions in modern organisms but had different functions in modern organisms' ancestors.

3. What are **adaptations**, according to the passage on page 54?

    A. traits that make an organism better able to survive in its environment
    B. traits that all members of a species possess
    C. traits that are learned and not inherited
    D. traits that appear only when two recessive alleles are inherited

4. The more similar the DNA of two species, the more closely related they are. Scientists have used modern DNA analysis to trace the evolutionary relationships among Darwin's 13 species of finches. DNA analysis revealed that the finch species all had very similar DNA. Thus, Darwin was correct when he proposed that they had evolved from a common ancestor.

    Which of the following best explains why DNA analysis provides better evidence to support the hypothesis that Darwin's finches evolved from a common ancestor than the scientific methods that Darwin used?

    A. DNA analysis takes less time than observation.
    B. DNA analysis is easier to do than observing birds in the wild.
    C. DNA analysis provides more objective data than observation does.
    D. Technological methods of obtaining evidence are inferior to observation.

Answers and explanations start on page 97.

LIFE SCIENCE

Organization of Ecosystems

An **ecosystem** is an area consisting of a community of organisms—plants, animals, fungi, bacteria—and the physical environment in which they live—soil, air, water, and climate. Earth as a whole is an enormous ecosystem called the **biosphere**. Smaller ecosystems include meadows, ponds, wetlands, and tidal zones. A healthy ecosystem contains a diversity of organisms. Some of the organisms, such as green plants, are called **producers** because they use energy from the sun to make their own food through photosynthesis. Other organisms, called **consumers**, depend on producers to meet their energy needs. These organisms eat plants, or eat organisms that eat plants, to get energy. The complex pattern in which energy passes through an ecosystem is called a **food web**. A simple food web for a wooded area is shown here.

Key Ideas

- An ecosystem is a community of organisms and their physical environment.
- Energy passes through an ecosystem from the sun, to producers (green plants), to consumers.
- Carbon, oxygen, nitrogen, and water cycle through the biosphere from the living to the nonliving components and back again.

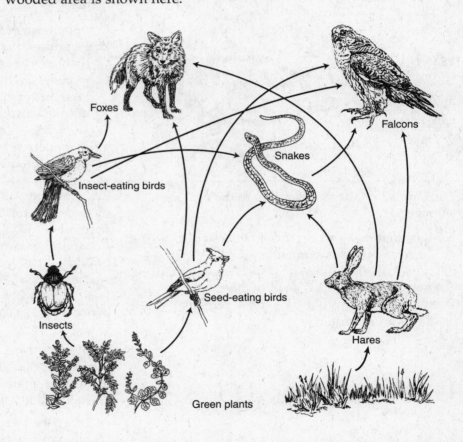

Foxes — Falcons — Snakes — Insect-eating birds — Insects — Seed-eating birds — Hares — Green plants

ON THE GED® TEST

On the GED® Science Test, you may see diagrams, like the one on this page, which contain arrows. Follow the directions of the arrows to understand the process.

Carbon, oxygen, nitrogen, and water also cycle through ecosystems from the living to the nonliving components and back again. As discussed in Lesson 2, carbon and oxygen cycle through the biosphere as a result of photosynthesis and cellular respiration. Nitrogen cycles between the land, organisms, and the air through chemical processes. Water cycles between the oceans and other surface water, the air, land, and organisms through evaporation, condensation, precipitation, and transpiration from plants.

PRACTICE 8

1. According to the passage, what is the ultimate source of energy for the food web on page 56?

   A. green plants
   B. mammals
   C. soil, air, and water
   D. the sun

2. Suppose most of the foxes in the woodland ecosystem on page 56 were hunted and killed. Which of the following is most likely to happen as a result?

   A. The amount of plant life in the woodland would increase.
   B. The populations of hares and seed-eating birds would increase.
   C. The populations of insects and insect-eating birds would decrease.
   D. The population of snakes would decrease.

3. Which of the following is most similar to a naturally occurring ecosystem?

   A. a diorama with dried vegetation and stuffed animals
   B. an aquarium with aquatic plants and herbivorous tropical fish
   C. a house with central air conditioning and heating
   D. a supermarket with a large section of fresh fruits and vegetables

4. In most cases, changes in one aspect of an ecosystem result in reactions in other parts of the ecosystem, restoring balance. In some cases, however, changes can be so great that the original ecosystem is replaced with another. When this occurs naturally, as when grasses are replaced by taller plants, shrubs, and eventually trees, it is called succession.

   Which of the following statements is supported by the information above?

   A. When changes are introduced into an ecosystem, its balance is permanently disrupted.
   B. Succession is usually caused by human destruction of an ecosystem.
   C. The intentional replacement of a wooded area by a field of cultivated wheat is an example of succession.
   D. The natural replacement of lichens by mosses and ferns, and then shrubs, is an example of succession.

5. Although more than three-quarters of the atmosphere is nitrogen, atmospheric nitrogen cannot be used directly by plants and animals. Instead, certain bacteria and blue-green algae take nitrogen from the air and, through a process called nitrogen fixation, turn it into compounds that plants can use. Nitrogen-fixing bacteria are found in the roots of some plants such as peas and beans. When these plants are present, the nitrate content of the soil is increased. Nitrates are absorbed by plants, which are eaten by consumers. Eventually the nitrogen returns to the soil in excrement and when organisms die.

   What is the role of nitrogen-fixing bacteria in the nitrogen cycle?

   A. to decompose dead plants and animals
   B. to add nitrogen to the atmosphere
   C. to turn atmospheric nitrogen into compounds plants and animals can use
   D. to take nitrogen from blue-green algae and turn it into compounds plants can use

Answers and explanations start on page 97.

LIFE SCIENCE PRACTICE QUESTIONS

1. Cell membranes are selectively permeable, allowing some substances to pass through and blocking others. The movement through the cell membrane takes place by means of passive or active transport. In passive transport, materials like water move through the cell's membrane without using any of the cell's energy. Active transport is the movement of materials in the cell from areas of low concentration to areas of high concentration. In active transport, the cell uses energy to move substances in and out. For example, transport proteins use energy when they carry molecules into and out of the cell.

What is the main difference between passive transport and active transport?

A. Active transport involves the passage of water, and passive transport does not.
B. Active transport requires the cell to use energy, and passive transport does not.
C. Active transport is used by animal cells, and passive transport is used by plant cells.
D. Active transport takes substances out of the cell, and passive transport brings them in.

2. Ben set up an experiment to prove that ivy plants take in water through their roots. He took a jar, put an ivy plant in the open jar, and filled the jar with water to cover only the roots of the ivy. After a week, he checked the water level in the jar and found it had gone down. Ben concluded that the plant had absorbed water through its roots.

Why does Ben have insufficient proof for his conclusion?

A. Ben should have put more ivy plants in the open jar.
B. Ben should have put several plants of different species in the open jar.
C. The water level in the jar might have gone down because of evaporation.
D. There should have been soil in the jar rather than water.

Questions 3 and 4 refer to the following information and diagram.

A pedigree shows the pattern of inheritance of a trait in a family. In a pedigree, circles represent females; squares represent males. A completely shaded shape indicates that the person has the trait. A half-shaded shape indicates the person carries the recessive form of the gene for the trait but does not have the trait. An unshaded shape indicates the person neither has nor carries the trait. In the following pedigree, Megan is a carrier of the genetic disorder cystic fibrosis, although she is healthy.

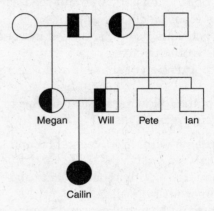

3. In the diagram above, one of Cailin's grandfathers is a carrier of cystic fibrosis. Circle that individual on the diagram.

4. Which of the following best explains why Megan's and Will's families were surprised to learn Cailin had inherited cystic fibrosis?

A. Megan and Will are carriers of cystic fibrosis.
B. Some of Will's distant ancestors had cystic fibrosis.
C. Megan's father and Will's mother are carriers of cystic fibrosis.
D. No one in either Megan's or Will's immediate family has cystic fibrosis except Cailin.

Questions 5 through 7 refer to the following paragraph and diagram.

Mitosis is a type of cell division in which two daughter cells are formed that have the same genetic material as the parent cell. Before mitosis starts, each chromosome in the nucleus duplicates itself to produce two sections, called chromatids, which are linked. Those chromatids then split, so that each daughter cell has DNA identical to that of the parent cell and to that of the other daughter cell. The function of the spindle fiber in mitosis is to control the movement of chromatids during mitosis. During the metaphase, for example, the spindle fiber helps to align the chromatids in a line across the middle of the cell so that the chromatids can divide evenly. The spindle fibers then direct the movement of the chromatids after they split, ensuring that each daughter cell has a full set of identical chromatids.

The Process of Mitosis

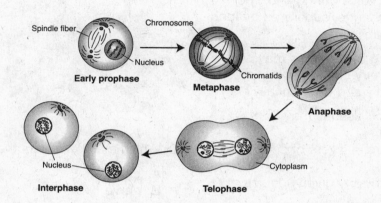

5. During which stage do the chromosomes line up across the middle of the cell?

   A. early prophase
   B. metaphase
   C. telophase
   D. interphase

6. Which of the following is true based on the paragraph and diagram?

   A. After mitosis, one of the resulting daughter cells is larger than the other one.
   B. After mitosis, the two daughter cells have their own nuclei.
   C. The first stage of mitosis is the division of the cell into two separate cells.
   D. The first stage of mitosis involves the formation of cytoplasm.

7. **Directions:** Use ten minutes to review the passage and diagram above, plan, and write a one- or two-paragraph response to the question below. Compose your answer on a computer if one is available, or write your answer on a separate sheet of paper. Include multiple pieces of evidence from the text to support your answer.

Spindle Fibers Writing Prompt

Explain why the function of the spindle fibers is important for the creation of identical daughter cells. Suggest an answer using multiple pieces of information from the paragraph and the diagram.

8. Charles Darwin thought that evolution took place gradually, with tiny changes eventually adding up to major change in a species. If this view is right, then there should be fossils, remains of long-dead organisms, that show the intermediate stages of evolution in a species. However, the fossil record often shows no intermediate forms for long periods of time. Instead, fossils of a species appear to suddenly become distinctly different. To account for this, some modern scientists have hypothesized that species evolve during short periods of rapid, major change, separated by long periods of relative stability.

Which of the following hypotheses may also explain why evolutionary change sometimes seems to occur rapidly and dramatically?

A. Organisms with soft tissues may form fossils.
B. Fossils usually form in layers of sedimentary rock.
C. The fossil record for any given species may be incomplete.
D. Fossils do not provide evidence for evolution.

9. Blood consists of blood cells and proteins suspended in a yellowish liquid called plasma. Red blood cells carry oxygen to the body. White blood cells protect the body against infection. Plasma transports nutrients and hormones to the body's cells and removes waste.

Which answer choice below describes some of the main functions of blood?

A. energy production and movement
B. movement and cell repair
C. cell repair and respiration
D. nutrient transport and immune defense

Questions 10 and 11 refer to the following diagram.

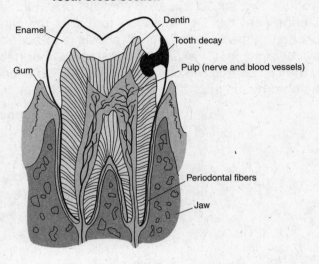

Tooth Cross Section

10. Which material covers the tooth's top surface?

A. enamel
B. nerve fibers
C. blood vessels
D. periodontal fibers

11. Tooth decay can eat away at the structure of a tooth. Tooth decay begins at the surface, but it must reach the pulp, which contains many nerve endings, before it will cause extreme pain. That suggests that the dentin contains [Select... ▾].

• few or no nerve endings
• many nerve endings
• more minerals than the enamel

12. The carrying capacity of an ecosystem is the maximum number of organisms it can support. If the carrying capacity is exceeded, there will not be enough resources, and one or more species will decline until a balance of organisms and resources is reached.

Which of the following is an example of people overloading the carrying capacity of an ecosystem?

A. using a park for recreation
B. grazing too many cattle on grassland
C. adding a room to a suburban house
D. banning shellfishing in polluted waters

13. Classification is the grouping of organisms based on similarities in their traits and their evolutionary histories. In the past, scientists classified organisms based primarily on a visual analysis of their structures and on the fossil record. Today, DNA analysis of selected genes is overturning many traditional classifications. For example, it was thought that sperm whales and dolphins, both of which have teeth, were closely related. However, DNA analysis revealed that sperm whales are actually more closely related to baleen whales, which do not have teeth.

What is the reason that DNA analysis has led to changes in the classification of organisms?

A. DNA analysis provides more fundamental, accurate data than does a visual analysis of structures and fossils.
B. Traditional classification was based on the erroneous assumption that organisms could be grouped by similarities.
C. When organisms possess similar structures, it always means that they are closely related.
D. When data from DNA analysis conflict with data from structural analysis, usually the structural data are correct.

14. *Homeothermy* refers to the maintenance of a constant body temperature in warm-blooded animals, such as dogs and human beings. Warm-blooded animals have specific body processes to help them gain or lose heat. For example, sweating helps cool the body through the evaporation of water, and shivering helps generate heat in cold environments.

Which of the following is most likely an example of a homeothermic process in dogs?

A. panting
B. healing after a wound
C. reproduction
D. grooming

Questions 15 through 17 refer to the following graph.

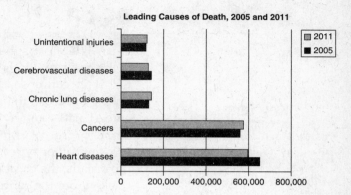

Source: National Center for Health Statistics

15. Provide a numerical response.

How many of the five causes of death depicted in the graph produced more deaths in 2011 than in 2005? _____

16. Compare the number of deaths from heart disease in 2005 to the number of deaths from heart disease in 2011. That difference represents the [Select... ▾] of all the causes of death depicted in the graph.

• biggest increase
• biggest decrease
• smallest increase

17. Which of the following approximately expresses the percentage change in deaths from heart diseases from 2005 to 2011? You MAY use your calculator.

A. 8% increase
B. 8% decrease
C. 92% increase
D. 92% decrease

Answers and explanations start on page 97.

EARTH AND SPACE SCIENCE

Structure of Earth

Earth is almost spherical, flattened at the poles, and bulging at the equator. It is composed of three main layers: the crust, the mantle, and the core. Earth's outer layer, its solid **crust**, is made of granite, basalt, gabbro, and other types of rock. Under the oceans, the crust is 3 to 6.8 miles thick; under the continents, the crust is from 12 to 40 miles thick. Below the crust is the molten **mantle**; it consists of silica and metal-rich minerals. The **core** has two layers: the outer core, which is mostly liquid iron, and the inner core, which is mostly solid iron. Extreme heat and pressure characterize the core.

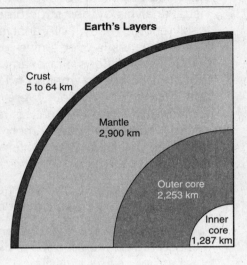

Earth's Layers

Crust
5 to 64 km

Mantle
2,900 km

Outer core
2,253 km

Inner core
1,287 km

The **theory of plate tectonics** explains phenomena of Earth's crust: seafloor spreading, the formation of major landforms, and the movement of continents. According to this theory, Earth's crust is made up of **tectonic plates** that fit together like a crude jigsaw puzzle. These plates move relative to one another at a rate of up to 15 centimeters (6 inches) a year. At the boundaries between plates, major landforms such as mountain ranges, volcanoes, ocean trenches, and mid-ocean ridges form, and earthquakes occur. There are three types of plate boundaries, or **margins**.

- At a **constructive margin**, two plates are moving apart and new crust is forming. Molten material from the mantle below wells up in the space between the plates, hardens, and forms new crust, usually at a mid-ocean ridge. For example, at the Mid-Atlantic Ridge, new crust is forming, causing the seafloor to spread and grow by about 5 centimeters (2 inches) a year.

- At a **destructive margin**, two plates are colliding and crust is being destroyed. When a continental plate collides with an oceanic plate, the denser oceanic crust may be forced under the other plate, forming a deep trench. When two plates consisting of continental crust collide, the crust crumples to form mountain ranges such as the Andes.

- At a **transform**, or **conservative**, **margin**, two plates are sliding by one another, and no crust is created or destroyed. For example, the San Andreas fault in California is the boundary between the North American plate and the Pacific plate, which is sliding northwest, causing many earthquakes.

As the plates move, they carry the continents with them. Scientists believe that a single large continent, **Pangaea**, existed about 250 million years ago. It gradually broke apart, and over millions of years the pieces (which are today's continents) drifted into the locations they are in today.

Key Ideas

- Earth is made up of three main layers: the crust, mantle, and core.
- The theory of plate tectonics explains how the seafloor spreads, how major landforms are created, and how the continents move.
- At the margins between plates, plates move away from or toward each other, or they slide past each other.

GED® TEST TIP

When you read a multiple-choice question, try to answer it before you read the choices. If one of the choices is similar to your answer, it is probably correct.

PRACTICE 1

1. What does the theory of plate tectonics explain?

   A. changes in Earth's crust
   B. changes in Earth's mantle
   C. changes in the composition of Earth's layers
   D. why there is extreme heat and pressure in Earth's core

2. Fill in the blanks with the options below.
   One similarity between Earth's inner and outer cores is that both (1) Select... , although the two are different because the inner core (2) Select... while the outer core (3) Select... .

Select (1)	Select (2)	Select (3)
consist primarily of iron	is mostly gaseous	is mostly gaseous
consist primarily of granite	is mostly liquid	is mostly liquid
consist primarily of silica	is mostly solid	is mostly solid

3. The Japan Trench off the coast of Japan is part of the boundary between an oceanic plate called the Pacific plate and a continental plate called the Eurasian plate. At the trench, the Pacific plate is forced beneath the Eurasian plate, causing earthquakes in Japan.

   The Japan Trench is an example of which type of crustal feature?

   A. a tectonic plate
   B. a mid-ocean ridge
   C. a constructive margin
   D. a destructive margin

4. Which of the following provides evidence that the present-day continents were once one large continent that broke apart?

   A. Australia is a large, continent-sized island.
   B. Eurasia is the largest land mass on Earth today.
   C. Australia and Antarctica are located in the Southern Hemisphere.
   D. The west coast of Africa seems to fit into the east coast of the Americas.

5. Which of the following is implied by the fact that seafloor spreading at the Mid-Atlantic Ridge is causing the Atlantic Ocean to widen by about 5 centimeters a year?

   A. The Mid-Atlantic Ridge is thousands of miles long.
   B. The Mid-Atlantic Ridge is the largest underwater structure in the Atlantic Ocean.
   C. The continents of North America and Europe are moving apart.
   D. The continents of North America and Europe are growing larger at the Mid-Atlantic Ridge.

6. Which of the following is a theory rather than a fact?

   A. The San Andreas fault is the boundary between the North American and Pacific plates.
   B. A single large landmass called Pangaea existed about 250 million years ago.
   C. The Earth's crust is composed of rocks like granite, basalt, and gabbro.
   D. Earthquakes often occur along tectonic plate boundaries.

Answers and explanations start on page 98.

EARTH AND SPACE SCIENCE

Earth's Resources

Key Ideas

- Natural resources include air, water, soil, minerals, and energy.
- Resources are either renewable (having an endless supply) or nonrenewable (having a limited supply).
- Conservation efforts limit the consumption, overuse, and pollution of the natural environment.

A **resource** is anything that is needed by humans to survive. Natural resources include air, water, soil, minerals, and energy. Air is involved in respiration, climate, and weather. Water is used for drinking, cooking, bathing, agriculture, and industrial processes. Less than 3 percent of the world's water is fresh water. **Soil** is the layer of loose disintegrated rock, organic matter, living organisms, air, and water in which rooted plants, including agricultural plants, grow. **Minerals** are the naturally forming inorganic substances with a crystalline structure of which rocks are made; they have many uses—from talcum powder to uranium fuel rods to diamond drill bits. **Energy resources** include fossil fuels, flowing water, wind, **solar energy**, and **geothermal energy**.

Resources can be classified as nonrenewable or renewable. **Nonrenewable resources** are those that take millions of years to form naturally; when they are used up, there is no replacement for them. For example, fossil fuels, including peat, coal, natural gas, and oil, are nonrenewable resources because they form over millions of years from decaying plant remains. Fossil fuels are our main source of energy for heating, transportation, and the generation of electricity. Soil and minerals are also nonrenewable resources.

Renewable resources are those whose supply will not run out, either because there is an unlimited supply, as is the case with **solar energy** (energy from the sun), or because the resource cycles through the environment, as is the case with water. In addition to solar energy, renewable energy resources include the water power of flowing rivers, tidal and wave power from the movement of ocean water, wind power from the movement of air, and geothermal power from the heat in the Earth's crust. All of these are used as alternative sources of energy to generate electricity.

People harm or destroy natural resources through consumption, overuse, and pollution. For example, some scientists estimate that we have already consumed between one-tenth and one-quarter of the world's supply of oil. Soil is subject to agricultural overuse and erosion. Air is polluted by fossil fuel emissions and its **ozone layer** is depleted by the release of compounds called chlorofluorocarbons (CFCs) into the atmosphere. Water is polluted by sewage, industrial waste, and agricultural and urban runoff.

Conservation is any action taken to preserve natural resources and protect the natural environment. Conservation involves a wide range of activities, including building more efficient combustion engines to reduce gasoline consumption; using catalytic converters to reduce the harmful emissions of burning fossil fuels; developing technologies to exploit renewable sources of energy; recycling glass, plastic, and metal wastes; using agricultural methods that protect the soil; building water treatment and sewage treatment plants; safely disposing of radioactive wastes; and cleaning up sites heavily polluted by industry.

PRACTICE 2

Questions 1 through 3 refer to the following graph.

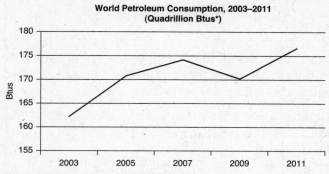

**World Petroleum Consumption, 2003–2011
(Quadrillion Btus*)**

Source: US Energy Information Administration
* Btus are British thermal units, a measure of energy

1. Approximately how many quadrillion Btus of petroleum were consumed in 2011?

A. 160
B. 170
C. 174
D. 177

2. Between its low point in 2003 and its high point in 2011, the approximate range of the data regarding world petroleum consumption was _____ quadrillion Btus.

* 10
* 14
* 176

3. Which of the following sentences best summarizes the information in the graph?

A. World petroleum consumption increased by about 14 quadrillion Btus between 2003 and 2011.
B. World petroleum consumption fell by about 4 quadrillion Btus between 2005 and 2009.
C. World petroleum consumption increased by roughly 50 percent between 2003 and 2007.
D. World petroleum consumption fell by roughly 50 percent between 2007 and 2009.

4. Which of the following proverbs best expresses the views of a conservationist?

A. All that glitters is not gold.
B. Every cloud has a silver lining.
C. Oil and water don't mix.
D. Waste not, want not.

5. The overall demand for water in the developed nations is rising. But it is not rising as quickly as people had predicted it would. In fact, the rate of water consumption per person per year in developed nations has actually dropped. This means that even though population has increased and industrial output has grown, the rate at which people withdraw water from reservoirs, rivers, and aquifers has slowed.

Which of the following is a likely reason for the drop in per person consumption of water in developed countries?

A. Vast new supplies of water have been found in the developed nations.
B. Developed nations have started using water more efficiently than they did in the past.
C. Developed nations are sharing water resources with each other.
D. Some developed nations export fresh water to other nations that lack it.

6. Soil erosion occurs when soil is worn away by the natural action of wind, water, and ice or by deforestation and poor farming practices. If soil erosion continues for a long time, it can lead to the formation of deserts. Some scientists estimate that the world lost about 20 percent of its farm topsoil between 1950 and 1990. Contour plowing, planting trees to serve as windbreaks, and other techniques can all reduce soil erosion.

Which of the following statements is supported by the information above?

A. All deserts originally formed as a result of soil erosion.
B. Most soil erosion is caused by poor farming practices.
C. Improved farming techniques can completely halt soil erosion.
D. Soil erosion is caused by both natural forces and the actions of people.

Answers and explanations start on page 99.

EARTH AND SPACE SCIENCE

Weather and Climate

Weather is the day-to-day change in conditions in the **atmosphere** at a particular place on Earth. **Climate**, on the other hand, is the average weather conditions of a large region over a long period of time.

All weather and climate ultimately arise from the uneven heating of the Earth. The sun's rays fall more directly at the equator than they do at the North and South Poles. This resulting uneven heating causes global wind circulation patterns: the warm air at the equator rises, creating an area of low pressure, and moves toward the poles. Cold air at the poles sinks, creating an area of high pressure, and moves toward the equator. The result is a pattern of **prevailing winds** in both the Northern and Southern hemispheres.

Global Wind Patterns

Another major influence on weather and climate, also caused by the uneven heating of Earth, is the worldwide pattern of **ocean currents**. Ocean currents are caused by the wind and by variations in the density of water (warm water is less dense than cold water). Ocean currents help transfer heat from the equatorial regions to the poles.

Daily weather patterns are caused by the movements of **air masses**, large bodies of air with similar temperature, humidity, and pressure. The boundary between two air masses is called a **front**. A **cold front** occurs where a cold air mass overtakes and displaces a warm air mass. A **warm front** occurs where a warm air mass rises over a cold air mass. An **occluded front** occurs when a cold front catches up with a warm front and the two weather systems merge. Clouds and **precipitation** are characteristic of fronts.

Meteorologists study the short-term weather patterns and data of particular areas. At meteorological stations around the world, temperature, humidity, cloud cover, wind, and other weather data are collected. Satellites and radar are also used to collect weather data. Weather predictions are based on comparing present weather conditions to computer models of previous weather conditions and storm systems in an area. When hurricanes, tornadoes, blizzards, or floods are forecast, meteorologists issue storm watches and warnings. For example, if a hurricane might reach an area in 24 to 36 hours, a hurricane watch is issued. If a hurricane is expected in an area in less than 24 hours, a hurricane warning is issued, and people are urged to take precautionary measures against the storm.

PRACTICE 3

Questions 1 through 4 are based on the information on page 66.

1. The diagram of global wind patterns on page 66 suggests that weather systems between 30°N and 60°N generally move in which direction?

   A. northeast to southwest
   B. northwest to southeast
   C. southeast to northwest
   D. southwest to northeast

2. Based on the diagram on page 66, how do the prevailing winds in the Northern Hemisphere compare to the prevailing winds in the Southern Hemisphere?

   A. The winds in the Northern Hemisphere blow faster than those in the Southern Hemisphere.
   B. The winds in the Northern Hemisphere are a mirror image of those in the Southern Hemisphere.
   C. The winds in the Northern Hemisphere blow east and those in the Southern Hemisphere blow west.
   D. The winds in the Northern Hemisphere blow west and those in the Southern Hemisphere blow east.

3. Hurricanes are violent storms with high winds and rain that form over the ocean. They cover an area 300 to 600 miles across and move relatively slowly—between 5 and 15 miles per hour. Meteorologists can now predict their paths with a great deal of accuracy.

   Which of the following technologies best accounts for accurate hurricane tracking?

   A. anemometers, which measure wind speed
   B. thermometers, which measure air temperature
   C. the Beaufort wind scale, a method of estimating wind speed
   D. satellites, which transmit cloud photos and weather data

4. Which of the following help even out the unbalanced heating of Earth as a whole?

   A. precipitation associated with fronts
   B. local air masses
   C. tornadoes, blizzards, and floods
   D. global wind and ocean current patterns

Questions 5 and 6 refer to the following chart.

Layers of the Atmosphere

Layer	Altitude	Temperature
Troposphere	0 to 6 miles	Average 59°F
Stratosphere	6 to 31 miles	−76°F to 32°F
Mesosphere and ionosphere	31 to 50 miles	32°F to −212°F
Thermosphere	50 to 435 miles	Up to thousands of degrees

5. For which of the following statements does the chart provide evidence?

   A. The higher you go in the atmosphere, the colder it gets.
   B. The higher you go in the atmosphere, the less oxygen there is to breathe.
   C. The highest layer of the atmosphere is the stratosphere.
   D. The highest temperatures in the atmosphere are in the thermosphere.

6. In the chart, draw a stick-figure inhabitant in the atmospheric layer in which most human activity takes place.

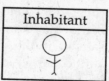

Inhabitant

Answers and explanations start on page 99.

EARTH AND SPACE SCIENCE

Earth in the Solar System

Key Ideas

- The solar system consists of the sun; the planets; their satellites, or moons; the asteroids; and the comets.
- There are eight planets: Mercury, Venus, Earth, Mars, Jupiter, Saturn, Uranus, and Neptune.
- The moon revolves around Earth every 27 days and appears to go through phases.

The **solar system** consists of the sun, a star; the **planets**; their **satellites**, or moons; the **asteroids**, sometimes called the minor planets; and the comets. The sun contains more than 99 percent of the **mass** (amount of matter) in the solar system, and all the other celestial bodies revolve around it, held by the force of **gravity**.

The eight planets of the solar system include (in order from the sun) Mercury, Venus, Earth, Mars, Jupiter, Saturn, Uranus, and Neptune. Mercury, Venus, Earth, and Mars are called the **inner planets** because they are relatively close to the sun. They are all small, rocky planets. Jupiter, Saturn, Uranus, and Neptune are called the **outer planets** because of their great distance from the sun. The outer planets are gas giants. Some facts about the planets are presented in the following chart.

The Planets of Our Solar System

Planet	Distance from sun	Diameter	Number of moons	Rotation period (day)	Revolution period (year)
Mercury	36 million mi	3,030 mi	None	59 Earth days	88 Earth days
Venus	67 million mi	7,500 mi	None	243 Earth days	225 Earth days
Earth	93 million mi	7,923 mi	1	23 hr 56 min 4.1 sec	365 days 5 hr 48 min 46 sec
Mars	142 million mi	4,210 mi	2	24 hr 37 min	687 Earth days
Jupiter	484 million mi	88,700 mi	50	9 hr 51 min	11.86 Earth years
Saturn	0.9 billion mi	75,000 mi	53	10 hr 14 min	29.46 Earth years
Uranus	1.8 billion mi	31,600 mi	27	17 hr 12 min	84 Earth years
Neptune	2.8 billion mi	30,200 mi	13	16 hr 7 min	164.8 Earth years

Earth is unusual among the planets in that about 70 percent of its surface is covered by water. It is the only celestial body in the solar system on which life is known to exist. Earth's rocky satellite, the moon, is the fifth largest satellite in the solar system. It has no atmosphere, but it does have some surface ice, which was discovered in 1998. The moon revolves around Earth once every 27 days. During the lunar month, the moon appears to go through a series of **phases**—changes in the proportion of its surface that is in shadow. The cycle of phases takes approximately 29 days. U.S. astronauts landed on the moon in several missions from 1969 to 1972, making it the only celestial body visited by crewed spacecraft.

PRACTICE 4

Questions 1 through 4 are based on the information on page 68.

1. According to the chart on page 68, which of the planets takes the shortest time to revolve, or complete its orbit, around the sun?

   A. Mars
   B. Saturn
   C. Neptune
   D. Mercury

2. According to the chart, which of the following planets is most similar to Earth?

   A. Mercury
   B. Venus
   C. Jupiter
   D. Neptune

3. Before 1781, the only planets that were known were the ones visible to the naked eye: Mercury, Venus, Mars, Jupiter, and Saturn. In 1781, William Herschel, an astronomer who made his own superb and powerful telescopes, discovered a strange "star" that appeared as a greenish disk rather than a point of light. A few nights later, he observed that this "star" had moved relative to the background of the other stars. Herschel realized he had discovered another planet. It was named Uranus, after the Greek sky god. Later it was found that Uranus had actually been observed at least 20 times before, as far back as 1690, but each time it had been identified as a star.

   Which of the following is an unstated assumption that could help account for the fact that Uranus was misidentified as a star prior to 1781?

   A. Uranus takes 84 earth years to revolve around the sun.
   B. The length of a day on Uranus is about 17 hours.
   C. Uranus was not clearly visible with the telescopes generally in use at the time.
   D. Uranus was not visible when it was on the other side of the sun.

4. According to the chart on page 68, which of the following planets has the most moons?

   A. Jupiter
   B. Saturn
   C. Uranus
   D. Neptune

5. According to some estimates, it would cost about ten times more to send a crewed mission to Mars to collect geologic samples and look for life than it would cost to send a robotic mission. Some people think that a human mission would yield much more relevant data, justifying the additional cost. Others think there is no scientific reason to send crewed missions, which are costly and risky, when robotic missions will do.

   Which of the following values is most likely to provide the motivation to send a crewed mission to Mars despite the risk and the additional cost?

   A. a desire to provide equal opportunities for astronauts of all nationalities
   B. a desire for economic development
   C. a desire to demonstrate the superiority of computers over humans
   D. faith in human judgment and decision-making skills

6. The structure of the solar system, with the massive sun at the center and many objects revolving around it, is most similar to the structure of which of the following?

   A. a DNA molecule, with its twisted spiral shape
   B. an atom, with a dense nucleus and electrons orbiting the nucleus
   C. the electromagnetic spectrum, with waves of different lengths and frequencies
   D. the planet Earth, with its layers of crust, mantle, and core

Answers and explanations start on page 99.

EARTH AND SPACE SCIENCE

The Expanding Universe

- Stars are globes of hydrogen and helium that produce their own heat and light through nuclear reactions.
- The sun is one star in the Milky Way galaxy, a large group of stars.
- The Big Bang theory helps explain the origin of the universe. According to this theory, the universe began as a compact spot of matter that exploded.

Our sun is a medium-sized yellow **star**, a globe of helium and hydrogen gas that produces its own heat and light through nuclear reactions. Stars like our sun generally have a 10-billion-year life cycle. They begin as **protostars**, which form from clouds of condensing gases and dust called **nebulae**. As a protostar reaches a certain density and temperature, nuclear reactions begin, releasing huge amounts of energy. At this point, the star is known as a **main-sequence star**, the longest stage in the stellar life cycle. After billions of years, the star begins to run out of hydrogen fuel. It may become a **red giant**. In time, the red giant becomes unstable and collapses, either exploding as a **supernova** and leaving behind a **neutron star** or losing mass slowly to become a **white dwarf**. A neutron star can be very dense, and gravity sometimes causes it to collapse in on itself, producing a **black hole**. Black holes are so called because their gravity is so great that light cannot escape from them.

The sun is just one star in a huge group of stars called the **Milky Way** galaxy. **Galaxies** consist of between one million and one trillion stars, along with clouds of gas and dust, which are held together by the force of gravity. Galaxies are classified according to their shape: spiral, barred-spiral, elliptical, and irregular. The Milky Way is a spiral galaxy. A spiral galaxy has a dense circular center with arms spiraling out from the core. Our solar system is located in one of the arms, called the Orion arm, of the Milky Way galaxy.

The Milky Way galaxy is part of a group of galaxies called the **Local Group**. There are 27 known galaxies in the Local Group, of which the Milky Way and the Andromeda galaxy are the largest.

The **universe** consists mostly of empty space with galaxies scattered throughout. Besides galaxies with stars at every stage of the life cycle, the universe has other bodies: **brown dwarfs** are objects that are less massive than a star but more massive than a planet; **pulsars** are thought to be rotating neutron stars that emit pulses of energy at regular intervals; and **quasars** are distant starlike objects that emit more energy than a hundred galaxies.

Cosmologists study the origin, properties, and evolution of the universe. One theory about the beginning of the universe is called the **Big Bang**. According to this theory, the universe began in a hot, superdense state smaller than an atom. The Big Bang caused all this compacted material to be flung outward, accounting for the still-expanding universe. There is evidence to support the Big Bang theory. First, galaxies appear to be moving away from one another in every direction, as if they had originated at a common point. Second, scientists have detected cosmic background radiation left over from the Big Bang. Cosmologists do not know what caused the Big Bang, but from the current rate of expansion of the universe, they estimate its age to be between 10 and 20 billion years.

PRACTICE 5

Questions 1 through 3 refer to the following paragraph and chart.

In astronomy, magnitude is an indication of the brightness of a celestial body. Magnitudes are measured along a scale from positive to zero to negative, with brightness increasing as magnitude decreases. Apparent magnitude is the brightness as seen from Earth, either by the naked eye or photographically. Absolute magnitude is a measure of the actual brightness of an object. It is defined as the apparent magnitude the object would have if it were located 32.6 light-years from Earth.

The Five Brightest Stars

Star	Distance from Earth (light-years)	Apparent magnitude	Absolute magnitude
Sirius	8.7	− 1.47	+ 1.41
Canopus	180	− 0.71	− 4.7
Alpha Centauri	4.3	− 0.1	+ 4.3
Arcturus	36	− 0.06	− 0.2
Vega	26	+ 0.03	+ 0.5

1. Choose information from the chart below to fill in the blanks. As seen from Earth, (1) [Select...▼] is the brightest star. However, if all the stars listed in the chart were 32.6 light-years from Earth, then (2) [Select...▼] would be brightest.

Select (1)	Select (2)
Sirius	Sirius
Canopus	Canopus
Alpha Centauri	Alpha Centauri
Arcturus	Arcturus
Vega	Vega

2. Which of the following would be true of a star with a position 32.6 light-years from Earth?

   A. The star's absolute magnitude would be less than that of Alpha Centauri.
   B. The star's apparent magnitude would be greater than its absolute magnitude.
   C. The star's apparent magnitude would be equal to its absolute magnitude.
   D. The star's apparent magnitude would be greater than that of Arcturus.

3. A magazine article makes the following statement about stars: A star's apparent magnitude and its absolute magnitude must always be close in value.

   Which of the following explains why the magazine's statement is incorrect?

   A. Stars form from huge masses of dust and gas.
   B. The absolute magnitude of a star indicates how bright the star looks to viewers on Earth.
   C. The apparent magnitude of a star is a measure of the amount of light the star puts out.
   D. Not all stars are located about 32.6 light-years from Earth.

4. The sun is about 4.7 billion years old. Based on the information on page 70, at which stage of its life cycle is the sun?

   A. It is a protostar.
   B. It is a main-sequence star.
   C. It is a neutron star.
   D. It is a white dwarf.

5. Pluto has a diameter of just 1,438 miles. It is made mostly of ice and frozen rock. It is very small and has an irregular orbit. It was originally classified as the ninth planet from the Sun, but it has been recategorized as a dwarf planet within the Kuiper belt.

   Which of the following is not a factual detail about Pluto?

   A. Pluto has a diameter of 1,438 miles.
   B. Pluto is made mostly of ice and frozen rock.
   C. Pluto has an irregular orbit.
   D. Pluto should be classified as a dwarf planet.

Answers and explanations start on page 100.

EARTH AND SPACE SCIENCE PRACTICE QUESTIONS

1. Tides are the twice-daily rise and fall of water along the shores of the oceans. Tides are caused mainly by the gravitational pull of the moon, and secondarily by the gravitational pull of the sun. The highest tides, called spring tides, occur when the sun, moon, and Earth are in line. Other high tides, called neap tides, occur when the sun and moon are at right angles with respect to Earth.

Which of the following statements is supported by the information above?

A. The moon and the sun exert the greatest pull on Earth's oceans when these bodies are all in a line.
B. When the moon is at right angles to the sun with respect to Earth, tides do not occur along the ocean shore.
C. Spring tides occur only in the spring, and neap tides occur only in the fall.
D. Neap tides are generally higher than spring tides.

2. Geothermal energy is energy extracted from naturally occurring steam, hot water, or hot rocks in Earth's crust. It is used to heat buildings and generate electricity in areas where hot magma (melted rock) is close to the surface.

In which of the following places is geothermal energy most likely to be used?

A. Arizona, a state where abundant sunshine provides solar energy
B. Cape Cod, a peninsula formed from glacial deposits of sand
C. Iceland, an island nation in the Atlantic with active volcanoes
D. Saudi Arabia, a Middle Eastern nation with ample oil and gas reserves

Questions 3 and 4 refer to the following paragraph and graph.

Scientists think there may be more matter and energy in the universe than has been directly observed because of some gravitational effects that cannot be explained otherwise. Dark matter and dark energy, so-called because they do not interact with light, may account for most of the stuff of the universe. In fact, ordinary matter, made of the chemical elements, may form only 4 percent of the universe.

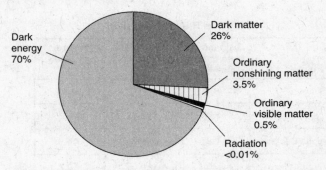

Source: Ostriker, Jeremiah and Paul Steinhardt, "The Quintessential Universe" *Scientific American,* January, 2001

3. According to the graph, about what percentage of the universe may consist of matter that does not interact with light?

A. less than 0.01 percent
B. 0.5 percent
C. 4 percent
D. 26 percent

4. Which of the following statements is a fact rather than a hypothesis about the makeup of the universe?

A. Dark energy may account for 70 percent of the universe.
B. Dark matter may account for 26 percent of the universe.
C. Dark energy may cause gravitational effects.
D. Ordinary matter is made of the chemical elements.

Questions 5 through 8 refer to the following map.

World Climate Zones

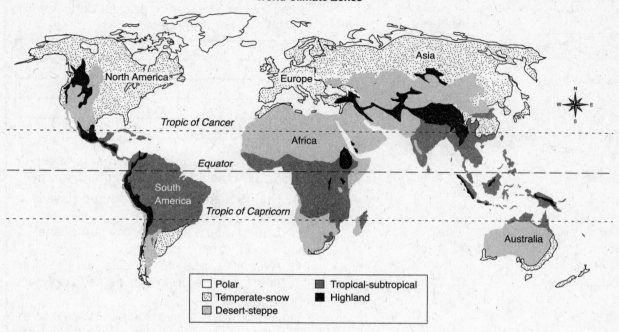

5. Which type of climate is characteristic of areas along the equator?

   A. polar
   B. temperate-snow
   C. desert-steppe
   D. tropical-subtropical

6. Which of the following statements is supported by information on the map?

   A. The continent with the least area of desert-steppe climate is Europe.
   B. Australia's climate is entirely tropical-subtropical.
   C. Africa and South America do not have areas with highland climate.
   D. Only North America has a large temperate-snow climate zone.

7. Temperate-snow climate zones hold only one-third of the world's people yet produce about two-thirds of the world's wealth. Historically, the fact that temperate-snow climate zones have more [Select... ▾] than other climate zones do is the most likely explanation for this discrepancy between population and productivity.

   • farm output
   • seasons
   • tropical rain forests

8. The continents shown above have, on average, how many different climate zones? Write your answer on the line below. You MAY use your calculator.

   _____

Questions 9 and 10 are based on the following diagrams.

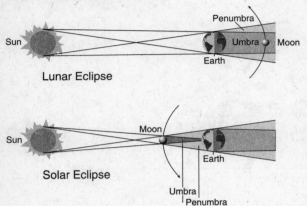

Lunar Eclipse

Solar Eclipse

9. Fill in the blanks using the options below. Based on the diagram, a lunar eclipse occurs when (1) [Select...▾] passes between (2) [Select...▾] and the sun.

Select (1)	Select (2)
the moon	the sun
the sun	Earth
Earth	the moon
the moon's umbra	the moon's penumbra

10. Which of the following statements is supported by the information in the diagram?

   A. During a solar eclipse, the sun passes through Earth's umbra.

   B. During a lunar eclipse, the sun passes through the moon's umbra.

   C. A lunar eclipse can be seen only at night and a solar eclipse can be seen only during the day.

   D. A maximum of five solar eclipses and thirteen lunar eclipses are possible during each year.

Questions 11 and 12 are based on the following passage.

Acid rain is a form of precipitation caused by the release of sulfur dioxide and nitrogen oxide into the atmosphere. Acid rain is comprised of a mixture of wet and dry deposition. If the acidic chemicals in the air blow into places with wet weather, the acids fall to the ground in the form of rain or fog, affecting plant and animal life. In drier climates, the acidic chemicals mix into dust or smoke, which will then fall to the ground or on trees or buildings. These deposits are later washed off by rainstorms. The addition of water to these chemicals makes the resulting mixture more acidic.

The acidic chemicals themselves form as a byproduct of burning fossil fuels, such as coal, oil, diesel, and gasoline. Acid rain alters the chemical balance of lakes, affecting aquatic life. It also alters the chemical balance of soil, harming plant life. In addition, it damages buildings and statues.

11. Which of the following technologies can help reduce acid rain?

   A. a diesel locomotive, which burns diesel fuel to produce energy that is used to turn the wheels

   B. an electric power plant that burns coal to heat water and produce steam to drive turbines, which power the generator

   C. a refinery, which purifies metals, petroleum, and other substances into a more useful form

   D. a catalytic converter, a device in the exhaust system of a vehicle that reduces harmful emissions from the engine

12. **Directions:** Use ten minutes to read, plan, and write a one- or two-paragraph response to this short-answer activity. Compose your answer on a computer if one is available or write your answer on a separate sheet of paper.

Acid Rain Writing Prompt

A certain pond has been affected by acid rain. Explain how it might be the case that the pond was affected by both wet deposition and dry deposition.

Questions 13 through 15 refer to the following diagram.

The Rock Cycle

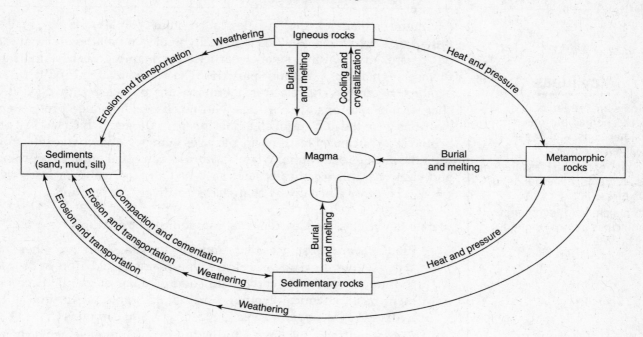

13. Which of the following statements is supported by the information in the diagram?

    A. The rock cycle is a continuous process of rock formation, destruction, and reformation.
    B. Sedimentary rocks form under conditions of heat and pressure.
    C. Metamorphic rocks form under conditions of compaction and cementation.
    D. Sediments form only from sedimentary rocks.

14. Fossils can form when plant or animal remains are buried under sand, mud, or silt. These materials can be compacted to form rock. A hiker knew she had found a(n) Select...▾ because it contained the fossilized imprint of a fish.

    • igneous rock
    • sedimentary rock
    • rock formed from magma

15. What is magma?

    A. melted rock
    B. crystallized rock
    C. cooled rock
    D. eroded rock

16. In open-pit mining, surface layers of soil and rock are stripped to obtain coal, ores, or minerals. It is cheaper than shaft mining because there is no underground work.

    Which of the following is the most likely reason that some countries restrict open-pit mining?

    A. There are no underground deposits.
    B. Open-pit mining is more dangerous than shaft mining.
    C. Open-pit mining destroys valuable land.
    D. Open-pit mining yields low-grade coal, ores, and minerals.

Answers and explanations start on page 100.

PHYSICAL SCIENCE

Atoms and Molecules

All matter is made of tiny particles called atoms. An **atom** is the smallest unit of matter that can combine chemically with other matter and that cannot be broken down into smaller particles by chemical means. Atoms are themselves made of **subatomic particles**. The major subatomic particles are protons, neutrons, and electrons. **Protons** are particles with a positive charge, and **neutrons** are particles with no charge. Together, protons and neutrons form the nucleus of all atoms except hydrogen, which has just one proton in its nucleus. **Electrons** are particles with negative charge. Electrons orbit the nucleus of an atom. When an atom has an equal number of protons and electrons, it is electrically neutral. When an atom gains or loses electrons, it becomes a negatively charged or positively charged **ion**.

Matter can be classified as elements, compounds, or mixtures.

- **Elements** are substances that cannot be broken down into other substances. They are made of a single type of atom. Gold, iron, hydrogen, sodium, oxygen, and carbon are some familiar elements. Each element has a **chemical symbol**. For example, gold is Au, iron is Fe, hydrogen is H, sodium is Na, oxygen is O, and carbon is C.
- **Compounds** are substances formed of two or more elements chemically combined in a definite proportion. Compounds have properties that differ from the properties of the elements that they contain. For example, at room temperature, water is a liquid compound made of the elements hydrogen and oxygen, which, uncombined, are both gases. Compounds are represented by **chemical formulas**. The chemical formula for water is H_2O, indicating that a water molecule is made of two atoms of hydrogen and one atom of oxygen.
- **Mixtures** are physical combinations of two or more substances that keep their own properties. For example, salt water is a mixture.

Key Ideas

- Atoms are formed of positively charged protons, neutral neutrons, and negatively charged electrons.
- All matter can be classified as elements, compounds, or mixtures.
- Atoms are held together in molecules and compounds by bonds.

GED® TEST TIP

If you are having trouble choosing the correct answer to a multiple-choice question, eliminate the options that are clearly wrong. Of the remaining options, choose the one that makes the most sense.

When elements combine to form **molecules** or ionic compounds, their constituents are held together by **bonds**. There are two main types of bonds: covalent and ionic. In a **covalent bond**, atoms share a pair of electrons, each atom contributing one electron. For example, the compound water is held together by covalent bonds. In an **ionic bond**, atoms gain or lose electrons to become ions, and the attraction between positively (+) and negatively (−) charged ions holds the compound together. For example, sodium chloride (NaCl), commonly called table salt, is an ionic compound.

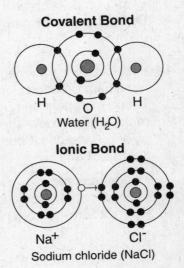

Covalent Bond

H   O   H

Water (H_2O)

Ionic Bond

Na⁺   Cl⁻

Sodium chloride (NaCl)

PRACTICE 1

Questions 1 through 3 are based on the information on page 76.

1. Sodium is represented by the chemical symbol Na and chlorine is represented by the chemical symbol Cl. According to the text and the diagram on page 76, what happens when sodium chloride forms?

   A. The sodium atom loses an electron, becoming positively charged, and the chlorine atom gains an electron, becoming negatively charged.
   B. The sodium atom gains an electron, becoming negatively charged, and the chlorine atom loses an electron, becoming positively charged.
   C. The sodium atom gains an electron, becoming positively charged, and the chlorine atom loses an electron, becoming negatively charged.
   D. The sodium and chlorine atoms share a pair of electrons, becoming ions and forming a covalent bond.

2. Water is composed of two atoms of hydrogen and one atom of oxygen and has the formula H_2O. Glucose, a simple sugar, consists of 6 atoms of carbon, 12 atoms of hydrogen, and 6 atoms of oxygen.

   Which of the following is the chemical formula for glucose?

   A. CHO
   B. $_6C_{12}H_6O$
   C. $C^6H^{12}O^6$
   D. $C_6H_{12}O_6$

3. Choose statements from the chart below to fill in the blanks.

   Based on the information on page 76, atoms are (1) Select... and ions are (2) Select... .

Select (1)	Select (2)
not necessarily either positively or negatively charged	not necessarily either positively or negatively charged
positively charged	positively charged
negatively charged	negatively charged
either positively or negatively charged	either positively or negatively charged

4. In 1911, British scientist Ernest Rutherford performed experiments that increased our knowledge of atomic structure. He bombarded an extremely thin sheet of gold foil with helium nuclei. (Helium nuclei, also called alpha particles, consist of two protons and two neutrons). He found that most of the helium nuclei passed right through the foil. Only a few were deflected back toward the source. On the basis of this experiment, Rutherford concluded that an atom has a dense nucleus with electrons orbiting it, but consists mostly of empty space.

   Which of the following is evidence that atoms consist mostly of empty space?

   A. Helium nuclei consist of two protons and two neutrons.
   B. Most of the alpha particles passed right through the gold foil.
   C. A few alpha particles were deflected off the gold foil and bounced back toward the source.
   D. Electrons orbit a dense nucleus consisting of protons and neutrons.

5. The number of protons in the nucleus of an atom is called the atomic number. Each element has a unique number of protons in its nucleus and therefore a unique atomic number.

   The atomic number of the element sodium is 11. How many electrons does a non-ionic sodium atom have?

   A. 10
   B. 11
   C. 12
   D. 22

Answers and explanations start on page 101.

PHYSICAL SCIENCE

Properties and States of Matter

Key Ideas

- Matter has mass and occupies space.
- The three states of matter include solid, liquid, and gas. A substance's state of matter can be changed by adding or removing heat.
- Solutions are a type of mixture. The solute is the dissolved substance. The solvent is what the solute is dissolved in. Solvents and solutes can be any of the states of matter.

Matter is anything that has mass and takes up space. The **mass** of an object is the amount of matter that it contains, and its **weight** is a measure of the gravitational force exerted on it. The mass of an object like a shovel never changes, but its weight can change. For example, a shovel weighs less on the moon than it does on Earth because the gravitational pull of the moon is less than that of Earth.

Under most conditions, there are three **states of matter**, as described below:

- **Solids** have a definite shape and volume because the molecules of which they are made occupy fixed positions and do not move freely. In some solids, such as minerals, the molecules form an orderly pattern called a **crystal**.
- **Liquids** have a definite volume but no definite shape because the molecules in a liquid are loosely bound and move freely. For this reason, a liquid conforms to the shape of its container.
- **Gases** have no definite shape or volume. The attraction between the molecules of a gas is very weak. In consequence, the molecules of a gas are far apart and are always in motion, colliding with one another and with the sides of the container.

The states of matter can be changed by adding or removing heat energy. When heat is applied to a solid, it melts. This happens because the motion of the solid's molecules increases until the bonds between them are loosened, allowing them to flow freely. The temperature at which a solid becomes a liquid is its **melting point**. When heat is applied to a liquid, it boils and evaporates, turning into a gas as the motion of its molecules increases. The temperature at which a liquid becomes a gas is called its **boiling point**. When heat is removed from a gas, the motion of its molecules decreases and it turns into a liquid. The temperature at which a gas becomes a liquid is its **condensation point**. When heat is removed from a liquid, the motion of its molecules slows until it solidifies. The temperature at which a liquid becomes a solid is its **freezing point**. The temperatures at which a substance changes state are unique properties of that substance. For example, water boils at 100°C (212°F) and freezes at 0°C (32°F). Water is also the only substance that is found naturally in all three states on Earth.

As you learned in Lesson 1, mixtures are physical combinations of two or more substances that keep their original properties. A **solution** is a mixture (such as salt water) that is uniform throughout and that contains ions, atoms, or molecules of two or more substances. The substance in a solution that is dissolved is called the **solute**. The substance in which the solute is dissolved is the **solvent**. In salt water, for example, salt is the solute and water is the solvent. Water is called the universal solvent because so many substances dissolve in it. However, solutions are not always liquids. They can be solids, as when two or more metals are combined in an **alloy**, or they can be gases, as when oxygen and nitrogen are combined in the air.

PRACTICE 2

Question 1 is based on page 78.

1. Which of the following physical changes involve adding heat to a substance?

   A. melting and boiling
   B. boiling and condensing
   C. condensing and freezing
   D. evaporating and condensing

2. Density is the amount of mass in a particular volume of a substance. It can be expressed in grams per cubic centimeter. The chart shows the densities of some common substances.

Densities of Substances

Substance	Density (g/cm³)
Solids	
Lead	11.35
Iron	7.87
Aluminum	2.70
Liquids	
Chloroform	1.49
Water	1.00
Ethyl alcohol	0.79
Gases	
Oxygen	0.0013
Nitrogen	0.0012
Helium	0.0002

Which of the following statements is supported by the information provided?

   A. Water is the least dense liquid on Earth.
   B. Solids are usually denser than liquids and gases.
   C. Density increases as the volume of a substance increases.
   D. Density decreases as the force of gravity decreases.

3. It is well known that the boiling point of water is 100° Celsius. More viscous, or thicker, substances often have higher boiling points. Glycerin, for example, boils at 290° Celsius, while olive oil boils at 300° Celsius.

   By what percentage is the boiling point of glycerin greater than that of water? You MAY use your calculator. Write your answer on the line below.

4. Water is different from most other substances. It changes from gas to liquid to solid at temperatures that are common on Earth. When it freezes, its molecules form a crystal lattice, so that its solid form is less dense than its liquid form. It is the most common solvent.

   Which of the following is a conclusion about water rather than a supporting statement?

   A. Water is a unique substance on Earth.
   B. Water changes state at temperatures typical on Earth.
   C. Frozen water is less dense than liquid water.
   D. Water is Earth's most common solvent.

5. When a solute is dissolved in a liquid solvent, the freezing point of the solution is lower than the freezing point of the pure liquid.

   In which of the following situations is this property of liquid solutions applied?

   A. Sugar dissolves in water more quickly if the solution is heated.
   B. Antifreeze added to water in a car's radiator lowers the freezing point below 0°C.
   C. The oil and vinegar in salad dressing is mixed more thoroughly by shaking.
   D. Spherical ice "cubes" freeze more quickly than regular ice cubes do.

6. A suspension is a mixture in which the distributed particles are larger than those of the solvent and in which the particles, in time, will settle out.

   Which of the following is a suspension?

   A. pure gold
   B. pure oxygen
   C. salt water
   D. dusty air

Answers and explanations start on page 101.

PHYSICAL SCIENCE

Chemical Reactions

Key Ideas

- In a chemical reaction, the atoms or ions of one or more reactants are rearranged, yielding one or more products. Mass is conserved during chemical reactions.
- Chemical reactions can be represented by chemical formulas.
- Chemical reactions are either endothermic or exothermic.

In a **chemical reaction,** the atoms or ions of one or more substances, called the **reactants,** are rearranged, resulting in one or more different substances, called the **products.** For example, iron, water, and oxygen react to form hydrated iron oxide, or rust. Matter is neither created nor destroyed during a chemical reaction, so the mass of the products always equals the mass of the reactants. This principle is known as the **law of conservation of mass**.

Chemical reactions can be represented by **chemical equations**. Chemical equations show the reactants on the left side and the products on the right side. They also show the proportions of the reacting substances—how many units of each reactant and each product are involved. Because of the law of conservation of mass, a chemical equation must balance. That is, the total number of atoms of an element on the left side must be equal to the total number of atoms of the element on the right side. Here is the chemical equation that represents the burning of hydrogen and oxygen to yield water.

$$2H_2 + O_2 \rightarrow 2H_2O$$

Restated in words: two molecules of hydrogen (H_2) combine with one molecule of oxygen (O_2) to form two molecules of water (H_2O). The equation balances because there are four hydrogen atoms on the left side and four on the right; there are two oxygen atoms on the left side and two on the right. To balance a chemical equation, you can change the coefficients—the number of units of any reactant or product. However, you *cannot* change the subscripts of any reactant or product.

Energy is involved in all chemical reactions. A reaction in which the reactants absorb energy from their surroundings is an **endothermic reaction**. For example, when you scramble an egg, you add heat energy and the egg solidifies. A reaction in which energy is given off with the products, usually in the form of heat or light, is an **exothermic reaction**. When you burn wood in a fireplace, for example, heat and light energy are given off. **Activation energy** is the amount of energy needed to get a reaction going. These energy relationships can be shown in graphs like those below.

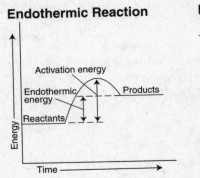

Endothermic Reaction

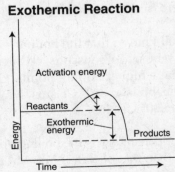

Exothermic Reaction

1. Which of the following chemical formulas represents the reaction in which copper (Cu) and oxygen gas (O_2) combine to form copper oxide (CuO)?

   A. $2CuO \rightarrow 2Cu + O_2$
   B. $Cu + O_2 \rightarrow 2CuO$
   C. $2Cu + O_2 \rightarrow 2CuO$
   D. $Cu + 2O_2 \rightarrow 2CuO$

2. Which of the following procedures would provide evidence for the law of conservation of mass?

   A. Weigh the reactants, conduct the reaction in an open container, and weigh the products.
   B. Weigh the reactants, conduct the reaction in a sealed container, and weigh the products.
   C. Measure the volume of the reactants, conduct the reaction in a sealed container, and measure the volume of the products.
   D. Write the chemical formula for the reaction and balance it.

3. Juanita would like to cook a scrambled egg on her gas stove. When she first turns on the stove's burner, the electronic ignition produces a spark that sets the gas burning. As the gas burns, it heats the frying pan. As the egg cooks, it absorbs the heat energy from the pan and solidifies.

   Match the correct form of energy needed with each step of Juanita's cooking process.

Juanita ignites the gas.	The gas burns.	The egg solidifies.

   Choices:

activation energy	endothermic energy

exothermic energy

4. In the graphs on page 80, what does the horizontal axis represent?

   A. the instant the reaction starts
   B. the instant the reaction stops
   C. the time during which the reaction occurs
   D. the energy level in the reaction

5. Organic compounds are those containing linked carbon atoms that form bonds with other atoms, usually hydrogen, oxygen, nitrogen, and/or sulfur. Organic compounds consist of chains, branching chains, rings, and other complex arrangements of carbon atoms with which other atoms bond. One type of organic compound is a polymer, a large long-chain or branching structure made up of many repeated simple units, called monomers. Natural polymers include cellulose. Synthetic polymers include polyethylene and other types of plastics.

   Which of the following is taken for granted and not stated by the writer of the paragraph above?

   A. Compounds are substances consisting of two or more elements chemically combined in a definite proportion.
   B. Organic compounds have linked carbon atoms forming bonds with other atoms, usually hydrogen, oxygen, nitrogen, and/or sulfur.
   C. Chains are among the arrangements carbon atoms in an organic compound can take.
   D. Plastics are synthetic polymers and cellulose is a natural polymer.

6. An acid is a compound that releases hydrogen ions (H^+), or protons, in the presence of water. Strong acids, like battery acid and stomach acid, are corrosive. Most dilute acids, like lemon juice, have a sour taste.

   A base is a compound that accepts hydrogen ions, or protons. Household cleaners like ammonia, lye, and bleach are bases. When an acid reacts with a base, the product is a salt and water. This reaction is called neutralization.

   Which of the following is the best title for this passage?

   A. "Corrosive Substances"
   B. "Acids and Bases"
   C. "Acids and Bases in the Lab"
   D. "Neutralization Reactions"

Answers and explanations start on page 101.

PHYSICAL SCIENCE

The Nature of Energy

Energy is defined as the capacity to do work. **Work** is done whenever a force is applied to an object to set it in motion. Thus, anything that can force matter to move, change direction, or change speed has energy.

Energy comes in many forms. **Heat energy** can change a solid to a liquid and a liquid to a gas. It is also involved in most chemical reactions. **Light energy** can create an image by causing the chemicals on a piece of film to react. It provides the energy needed for the process of photosynthesis in green plants. **Electrical energy** can turn a motor, plate a set of flatware with a layer of silver, or store data on a hard drive. **Chemical energy** in food provides the energy humans need for life functions. It heats our buildings when we burn oil, gas, coal, or wood. Chemical energy in batteries provides electricity when the batteries are connected in a circuit. **Nuclear energy** from breaking apart the nuclei of atoms provides energy to produce electricity or power a submarine. **Mechanical energy** turns the axles of a car or the blades of a fan.

Energy can be converted from one form to another. Consider the production and use of electricity. In most electric plants, a fossil fuel (chemical energy) is burned, producing heat energy that turns water to steam. The energy in the steam turns the blades of a turbine, producing mechanical energy. The turbine powers the generator, which produces electrical energy. Electrical energy is used in homes to provide heat energy (in stoves and toasters), light energy (in light bulbs), sound energy (in the stereo), and mechanical energy (in a blender). Even though energy undergoes changes in form, the amount of energy in a closed system remains the same. This principle is known as the **law of conservation of energy**.

Two basic types of energy are **potential energy** and **kinetic energy**. An object has potential energy because of its position; it has kinetic energy when it moves. For example, when you raise a hammer, at the top of your upswing the hammer has potential energy. When you lower the hammer to hit a nail, the hammer has kinetic energy, the energy of motion. When the hammer hits the nail, it transfers energy to the nail. The energy transferred is equal to the work done by the hammer on the nail, and it can be measured in **joules**. The rate of doing work or consuming energy is called **power**, and it can be measured in horsepower (in the English system) or **watts** (joules per second in the metric system).

Physicist Albert Einstein discovered the relationship between energy and mass and expressed it in the equation $E = mc^2$, in which E represents energy, m represents mass, and c represents the speed of light. Since the speed of light is a very large number, the equation indicates there is a great deal of energy in even the tiniest bit of matter. So, for example, in nuclear bombs and nuclear power plants, mass is changed to energy when large atoms are split into two or more smaller atoms with less mass than the original large atom.

Key Ideas

- Anything that can force matter to move, change direction, or change speed has energy.
- Energy comes in many forms and can be converted from one form to another.
- The law of conservation of energy states that energy can neither be created nor destroyed, only changed in form.

ON THE GED® TEST

Since many Science Test questions are based on diagrams and graphs, it is important to carefully read the titles and all of the other information on all graphics. Make sure you understand a graphic before answering questions based on it.

PRACTICE 4

Questions 1 through 4 are based on the information on page 82.

1. Which of the following states the law of conservation of energy?

   A. Potential energy is the energy of position; kinetic energy is the energy of motion.
   B. Energy can be created and destroyed as well as changed in form.
   C. Energy cannot be created or destroyed, but can only change in form.
   D. Energy cannot be created, destroyed, or changed in form.

2. During a power outage, George relied upon his flashlight to move around his home. The flashlight is constructed with wires and a lightbulb enclosed in a plastic casing. It requires batteries to operate.

   Write in the three types of energy involved in turning on and using the flashlight.

   Options:

sound	light
nuclear	electrical
chemical	

3. An oak tree may grow very tall very slowly. It may take the tree a hundred years to absorb light energy and store it as chemical energy, yet only a single winter to be turned into heat energy in someone's wood stove. Which concept does this fact best relate to?

   A. work
   B. power
   C. force
   D. kinetic energy

4. What does Einstein's equation $E = mc^2$ express?

   A. the relationship between electricity and magnetism
   B. the relationship between energy and mass
   C. the speed of light in a vacuum
   D. the relationship between electrical energy and nuclear energy

Question 5 refers to the following diagram.

A Pendulum's Energy

1. Pendulum has only potential energy
2. Pendulum has only kinetic energy
3. Pendulum has only potential energy

5. Which of the following statements is supported by the information in the diagram?

   A. At the high point of its swing, a pendulum has kinetic energy.
   B. At the high point of its swing, a pendulum has potential energy.
   C. As a pendulum swings through one arc, it loses all its energy.
   D. A pendulum can swing forever because of kinetic energy.

6. Heat energy is present in all matter in the form of the kinetic energy of its atoms and molecules. Heat energy can pass from one place to another through conduction: the transfer of kinetic energy from molecules in greater motion (hot areas) to molecules of lesser motion (cold areas). Solid metals like silver and copper are good conductors of heat energy; gases like air are poor conductors.

   What is the reason that air is a poor conductor of heat?

   A. The molecules in air are far apart.
   B. The molecules in air are very large.
   C. The molecules in air do not move.
   D. The molecules in air are very small.

Answers and explanations start on page 102.

PHYSICAL SCIENCE

Motion and Forces

Key Ideas

- Speed is the rate at which an object moves; velocity is speed in a given direction; acceleration is the rate at which velocity changes.
- A force is anything that changes the state of rest or motion of an object.
- Newton stated three laws of motion that explain the inertia, acceleration, and momentum of objects.

GED® TEST TIP

If you are asked to apply a general law or principle of science to a particular situation, ask yourself: "What is similar about this situation and the general principle?"

Everything in the universe is in motion. Even objects that seem to be at rest, like a building, are moving with Earth's rotation. **Speed** is the rate at which an object moves; **velocity** is its speed in a particular direction. **Acceleration** is the rate at which velocity changes. So a car's speed may be 40 miles per hour; its velocity may be 40 miles per hour toward the north; and it may accelerate by 10 feet per second until its velocity is 50 miles per hour to the north. A **force** is anything that tends to change the state of rest or motion of an object. A push or a pull on an object is a force, as are gravity and friction. So, for example, if you allow a car to coast on a level road, the force of friction will eventually bring it to a stop.

Sir Isaac Newton (1642–1727), an English physicist and mathematician, set down three laws by which the planets and all other objects move when acted upon by a force. These are called the **laws of motion**.

Newton's first law of motion, the **law of inertia**, states that an object at rest will stay at rest until a force acts upon it, and an object in motion will stay in motion at a constant speed in a straight line until a force acts upon it. Objects moving on Earth eventually slow down and stop because of the forces of friction and gravity. A bullet, for example, would continue its forward motion in a straight line, but friction from the air slows it down and the force of gravity pulls it toward the ground.

The second law of motion, sometimes called the **law of motion** or **acceleration**, states that the acceleration of an object depends on its mass and the force acting upon it. The greater the force, the greater the acceleration. The more massive the object, the more force it takes to accelerate it. Additionally, if a constant force acts upon an object, the object will move with constant acceleration in the direction of the force. This is why truck engines are more powerful than car engines: it takes more force to accelerate an object with more mass (a truck) than an object with less mass (a car).

Newton's third law of motion states that for every action, there is an equal and opposite reaction. This law was used to derive the law of conservation of momentum. **Momentum** is related to the amount of energy that a moving object has, and it depends on the mass of the object and its velocity. In fact, momentum is defined as an object's mass multiplied by its velocity. Newton's third law states that when an object is given a certain amount of momentum in a particular direction, some other object must receive an equal momentum in the opposite direction. Another way to state this is to say that all forces exist in pairs, and that all forces are interactions between objects. So, for example, when a bullet is fired out of a gun, the bullet's forward momentum causes the gun to recoil, or move backward.

PRACTICE 5

<u>Questions 1 through 3 are based on page 84.</u>

1. What is a force?

   A. the rate at which an object moves in a particular direction
   B. any change in an object's acceleration or deceleration
   C. the inertia and momentum of an object at rest
   D. anything that changes the rest or motion of an object

2. What is inertia?

   A. the speed at which an object is moving
   B. changes in an object's speed or direction
   C. the force needed to move an object a certain distance
   D. the tendency of an object to remain at rest or in motion

3. The force that is needed to keep an object moving in a circular path is called centripetal force.

   Which of the following is an example of motion that requires centripetal force?

   A. the tides occurring as a result of the moon's gravitational pull
   B. the International Space Station orbiting Earth
   C. a parachute slowing as it falls to the ground
   D. a gun recoiling as a bullet is fired

---

4. Select the phrase from the choices below that correctly completes the paragraph.

A car is traveling at a velocity of 30 miles per hour across a narrow bridge when it is approached on a collision course by another car traveling at 30 miles per hour. The momentum of each car is propelling it forward, and there is no way to completely avoid an impact. Because the momentum of the car `Select... ▼`, each driver should attempt to decrease his car's speed to lessen the severity of impact.

   • decreases when its velocity decreases
   • increases when its velocity increases
   • decreases when its velocity increases

<u>Question 5 refers to the following graph, the paragraph below, and the information on page 84.</u>

Graphs are often used to convey information about motion. One type of motion graph shows distance and time. Distance is measured from a particular starting point. If the distance graph has a straight, horizontal line, the distance is unchanging and the object is not moving. If the distance graph has a straight line with an upward slope, the distance is changing at a constant rate; this means that the object is moving at a constant speed. If the distance graph is a curve, the object is accelerating or decelerating, depending on the shape of the curve.

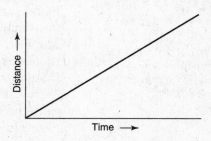

5. What does the graph above show?

   A. an object that is not moving
   B. an object that has a constant speed
   C. an object that is accelerating
   D. an object that is decelerating

---

6. A machine is a device that transmits a force, changing the direction or size of the force and doing work. The force applied to a machine is the effort force; the force it overcomes is the load. Types of simple machines include the inclined plane, wedge, lever, pulley, and wheel-and-axle.

   Which of the following statements is supported by the information given?

   A. The force a machine overcomes is called the effort force.
   B. Work can be done only with machines.
   C. Some machines simply change the direction of a force.
   D. All machines change both the direction and size of a force.

Answers and explanations begin on page 102.

PHYSICAL SCIENCE

Electricity and Magnetism

Key Ideas

- Particles with like electric charges repel one another, and particles with unlike electric charges attract one another.
- The flow of electrons through a substance is called an electric current.
- An electric current produces a magnetic field, and a moving magnetic field produces an electric current.

As you recall from your study of atoms, electrons have a negative charge (−), and protons have a positive charge (+). This **electric charge** causes them to exert forces on one another. Particles with like charges repel one another, and particles with unlike charges attract one another. Sometimes electrons are temporarily pulled away from atoms, creating stationary areas of positive and negative charge. This can happen when two objects, like a balloon and a rug, are rubbed together, creating **static electricity**.

The movement of charged particles, usually electrons, is an **electric current**. Direct current flows in one direction only, and it is used in battery-operated devices. Alternating current flows back and forth rapidly, and it is used in household wiring. A material that allows electrons to move freely from atom to atom is called a **conductor**. Metals are good conductors. A material that does not allow electrons to move freely from atom to atom is called an **insulator**. Rubber and plastic are examples of insulators. **Semiconductors** are substances whose ability to conduct electricity is midway between that of a conductor and an insulator. Semiconductors like silicon are used in electronic devices.

An electric current produces a **magnetic field** that affects magnetic substances such as iron in the same way a permanent magnet does. Magnetic fields are produced by moving charged particles. In an **electromagnet**, the charged particles move along a coil of wire connected to a battery or other power source. In a **permanent magnet**, the spinning of electrons creates a magnetic field. Every magnet has two ends, called the north and south poles. The north pole of one magnet attracts the south pole of another magnet; like poles repel one another.

Magnetic Fields

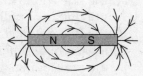

Bar magnet

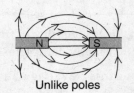

Unlike poles

Like poles

Just as an electric current produces a magnetic field, a moving magnetic field produces an electric current. This principle underlies electric motors, generators, and transformers. In an **electric motor**, for example, magnetic fields are produced by electric currents. The magnetic fields push against one another, turning the shaft of the motor. In a **generator**, a moving magnetic field produces electric current. In a **transformer**, an incoming electric current in coiled wire produces fluctuating magnetic fields, which in turn produce an outgoing electric current of a different **voltage**. The difference in voltage is caused by the differing sizes of the wire coils.

PRACTICE 6

Questions 1 through 3 are based on page 86.

1. Suppose a drawing of two magnets with their north poles facing one another were added to the diagram on page 86. What would the new drawing show?

   A. two poles attracting one another
   B. two poles repelling one another
   C. magnetic lines of force connecting the poles
   D. magnetic lines of force flowing southward

2. What is the reason copper and aluminum are used for electrical wiring?

   A. Copper and aluminum are conductors.
   B. Copper and aluminum are insulators.
   C. Copper and aluminum are semiconductors.
   D. Copper and aluminum are magnetic.

3. Based on the information on page 86, which of the following devices is most likely to use direct current?

   A. a washing machine
   B. a desktop computer
   C. a toaster
   D. a flashlight

4. In an electric power plant, generators may produce electric current at about 10,000 volts. The current may be stepped up and transmitted along high voltage lines at 230,000 volts, and then stepped down to about 2,300 volts for transmission in a city. Finally, before it enters houses, the current is stepped down to 110 volts.

   Based on the information above and that on page 86, which of the following devices steps current up and down for efficient transmission?

   A. a conductor
   B. an electromagnet
   C. an electric motor
   D. a transformer

Questions 5 and 6 refer to the following paragraph and diagram.

An electric circuit is a complete pathway for the flow of electric current. It consists of a source of electricity, such as a battery, wires along which the current travels, devices called resistors powered by the current, and often a switch to start and stop the flow of current.

A Series Circuit

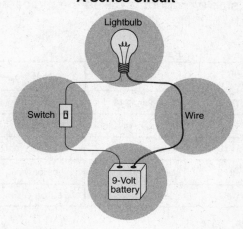

5. Circle the element of the diagram that acts as a resistor in the circuit.

6. A student was asked how the current in the circuit shown above could be stopped without using the switch. He answered that the only way to stop the current was to disconnect the battery.

   What was wrong with the student's response?

   A. Disconnecting the battery will not stop the current.
   B. Removing the fuse will also stop the current.
   C. Disconnecting the lightbulb will also stop the current.
   D. There is no way to stop the current without using the switch.

Answers and explanations start on page 102.

PHYSICAL SCIENCE PRACTICE QUESTIONS

Questions 1 and 2 refer to the following paragraph and chart.

When the nuclei of unstable elements disintegrate, emitting radioactive radiation, the unstable elements change into other elements, becoming more stable. The amount of time it takes for half of a sample of a radioactive element to decay into its stable product is called the radioactive element's half-life.

Radioactive Decay

Radioactive element	Decays into	Half-life
Radon-222	Polonium-218	3.82 days
Carbon-14	Nitrogen-14	5,730 years
Uranium-235	Lead-207	713 million years
Uranium-235	Lead-206	4.5 billion years
Rubidium-87	Strontium-87	50 billion years

1. What is the half-life of carbon-14?

   A. 3.82 days
   B. 5,730 years
   C. 713 million years
   D. 4.5 billion years

2. Uranium is used as fuel in nuclear power plants, resulting in radioactive waste, which is dangerous to living things.

   Which of the following arguments is likely to be used by opponents of nuclear power?

   A. Uranium is a plentiful source of fuel for generating electricity.
   B. Uranium is a renewable resource, and therefore its use is limitless.
   C. During the three days that radioactive waste is unstable, it may harm living things.
   D. Uranium produces radioactive waste that may harm living things for millions of years.

Questions 3 and 4 refer to the following paragraph and diagram.

An oscillation is a back-and-forth or up-and-down movement. When an oscillation travels through matter or space and transfers energy, it is called a wave.

Longitudinal Wave

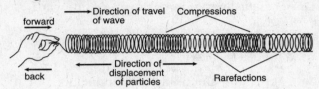

Transverse Wave

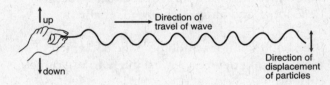

3. What is the main similarity between longitudinal and transverse waves?

   A. Both involve up-and-down displacement of particles.
   B. Both involve back-and-forth displacement of particles.
   C. Both involve compressions in which particles are pushed together.
   D. Both involve the transfer of energy through matter or space.

4. After a transverse wave passes through a substance, no particle ever ends up far from its original position.

   Which of the following illustrates this principle?

   A. A cork in water bobs up and down as waves pass.
   B. Sound waves travel through air.
   C. When two waves overlap, they interfere with one another.
   D. A stone dropped into a pond causes ripples to radiate outward.

5. According to the kinetic theory of matter, all matter is made up of molecules in a state of constant motion. The motion of molecules can be inferred by observing particles in a fluid (a liquid or a gas) as they are hit by molecules of the fluid. The random, zigzag movement of the particles is called Brownian motion.

Which of the following is an example of Brownian motion?

A. dust motes dancing in a shaft of sunlight
B. the ground vibrating as a truck passes
C. water evaporating from a puddle
D. an inflatable raft floating on a lake

6. In a chemical reaction, the surface area of the reactants affects the rate at which the reaction occurs. The greater the surface area of the reactants, the faster the reaction rate will be.

When dilute sulfuric acid reacts with marble, carbon dioxide gas is produced. Among the options below, one will increase the rate of reaction, and one will decrease the rate of reaction. Match the appropriate action to the corresponding box for each effect—increasing and decreasing the rate of reaction.

Increase Rate of Reaction	Decrease Rate of Reaction

Options:

Use a larger container.	Use a smaller container.
Use powdered marble.	Use larger chunks of marble.

7. Boyle's law states that at a constant temperature, the volume of a fixed amount of gas varies inversely with the pressure exerted on the gas. Therefore, the volume of a gas [Select...▾] when the pressure on the gas increases.

- increases
- decreases
- remains the same

Questions 8 and 9 refer to the following paragraph and chart.

All of the elements are arranged in the periodic table according to atomic number—the number of protons in an atom of each element. The rows of the periodic table show elements according to the structure of their electron orbits. The columns, or groups, show elements with similar properties. A portion of the periodic table is shown below.

Part of the Periodic Table

13	14	15	16	17	18
					He 2
B 5	C 6	N 7	O 8	F 9	Ne 10
Al 13	Si 14	P 15	S 16	Cl 17	Ar 18
Ga 31	Ge 32	As 33	Se 34	Br 35	Kr 36
In 49	Sn 50	Sb 51	Te 52	I 53	Xe 54
Tl 81	Pb 82	Bi 83	Po 84	At 85	Rn 86

8. Group 18 is also called the noble gases. Their electron orbits are completely filled, and they rarely react with other elements. Which of the following is a noble gas?

A. nitrogen (N)
B. chlorine (Cl)
C. xenon (Xe)
D. fluorine (F)

9. Which of the following statements is supported by the information given?

A. Silicon (Si) is a very common element.
B. Chlorine (Cl) and iodine (I) have similar properties.
C. Arsenic (As) and antimony (Sb) have very different properties.
D. Arsenic (As) has 85 protons in its nucleus.

Electromagnetic radiation consists of electric and magnetic fields that oscillate back and forth. There is a wide range of types of electromagnetic radiation, which together form the electromagnetic spectrum.

The Electromagnetic Spectrum

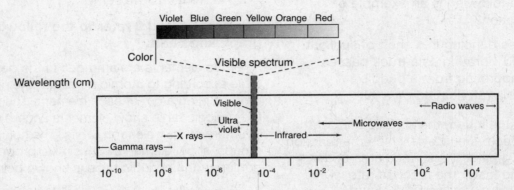

10. Which of the following types of electromagnetic radiation has a wavelength longer than those in the visible spectrum?

    A. microwaves
    B. ultraviolet light
    C. X-rays
    D. colored light

11. Which of the following generalizations is supported by the diagram?

    A. Unlike people, some insects can see ultraviolet light.
    B. Warm colors like yellow have a shorter wavelength than cool colors like blue.
    C. People can see only a small portion of the electromagnetic spectrum.
    D. In medicine, X rays are used to make images of bones.

12. Objects are attracted to one another by the force of gravity. Gravity is proportional to the mass—the amount of matter—objects have; gravity decreases as the distance between the objects increases. An object's weight is a measurement of the Earth's gravitational pull on the object.

    What happens to the mass and weight of a rocket as it travels beyond Earth's orbit?

    A. Its mass remains the same, and its weight increases.
    B. Its mass remains the same, and its weight decreases.
    C. Its mass decreases, and its weight decreases.
    D. Its mass increases, and its weight remains the same.

13. Heat energy can be transferred from one object to another. In summer, when you hold an ice-cold can of soda against your face, your face feels cooler. However, what is really happening is that the can is being warmed by heat from your body. You are actually losing a little body heat.

    Which of the following is an unstated assumption related to the paragraph?

    A. Heat can be transferred.
    B. Coldness cannot be transferred.
    C. A cool object can be warmed by your body.
    D. You can lose body heat.

Questions 14 and 15 refer to the following table and paragraph. You MAY use your calculator.

An aviation engineer tests five newly developed airplanes by measuring and recording the top speed of each plane. Unbeknownst to the engineer, the radar she used to measure the planes' speeds is faulty: it gives the speed of any object in motion as 3.7 km/hour faster than it really is. The following table shows the speeds that the engineer recorded using the faulty radar and the actual speed of each plane:

Airplane	Recorded speed (km/hour)	Actual speed (km/hour)
1	214.4	210.7
2	362.1	358.4
3	410.0	406.3
4	214.4	210.7
5	359.6	355.9

Using the speeds recorded from the faulty radar, the engineer then calculated the mean, median, mode, and range of the planes' speeds.

14. Which one of the engineer's calculations using the recorded speed is identical to what it would have been had the engineer made the same calculation using the actual speed of each plane?

    A. the mean
    B. the median
    C. the mode
    D. the range

15. After completing her measurements, the engineer selects at random two planes to demonstrate at an upcoming air show. What is the probability that the actual speeds of both planes selected are less than 360 km/hour?

    A. $\dfrac{1}{5}$

    B. $\dfrac{3}{10}$

    C. $\dfrac{3}{5}$

    D. $\dfrac{4}{5}$

Directions: Use ten minutes to read the following passage, plan, and write a one- or two-paragraph response to the question below. Compose your answer on a computer if one is available or write your answer on a separate sheet of paper. Include multiple pieces of evidence from the text to support your answer.

16. A pharmaceutical company sells a popular decongestant in capsule form. Market research shows that a new product combining the decongestant with the company's most popular pain reliever and sold in liquid form would be a big seller during cold and flu season. One problem is that the decongestant is extremely bitter when dissolved in water and the proposed product would require a flavor to be added to make it palatable to customers. The company tested several flavors and found that customers preferred a particular cherry flavor to all others. When the company's chemists created a sample of the decongestant, the pain reliever, and the cherry flavor, however, they discovered that the resulting compound coagulated into a liquid too thick to be easily swallowed. Chemist A hypothesized that the problematic ingredient was the pain reliever and suggested that the decongestant, the flavor, and an alternative pain reliever could be combined into a successful product. Chemist B disagreed; she suggested that the flavor was the ingredient causing the product to thicken and that a new flavor should be substituted into the product along with the popular decongestant and the popular pain reliever.

Decongestant Writing Prompt

Describe an experiment or series of experiments that the chemists could conduct to determine which of the chemists' hypotheses is correct or whether they are both wrong and further research is needed for the proposed product.

Answers and explanations start on page 103.

PRACTICE QUESTIONS ANSWERS AND EXPLANATIONS

Science Practices

Lesson 1: Comprehend Scientific Presentations

Practice 1, page 27

1. **C. The causes of type 2 diabetes** The passage as a whole discusses the causes of type 2 diabetes. Choices (A) and (D) are not discussed in the passage. Choice (B) is mentioned in the second paragraph but is only a supporting detail.

2. **D. The causes of type 2 diabetes are not fully understood.** This question asks for the main point of just the first paragraph, which explains that scientists do not fully understand the role played by various factors in causing diabetes. Choices (A) and (B) both commit the same error: that is, they mention a specific detail from the first paragraph while missing the big picture. Choice (C) contradicts the paragraph.

3. **B. A study of 18- to 25-year-olds showed that a majority did not produce enough insulin to offset the high amounts of sugar they were consuming.** The question asks for a detail that serves to support the idea that high sugar consumption may contribute to the development of type 2 diabetes. Only choice (B) does so. Choice (A) is a detail that is indeed mentioned in the paragraph, but only as background information. It does not serve to support the author's point that sugar consumption may contribute to diabetes. Choice (C) brings in "genetic factors," which are not mentioned in paragraph two. Although choice (D) may be implied by the author's use of hesitant language, such as "one contributing factor *may* be high sugar consumption," this does not support the paragraph's main idea.

4. **A. As moist, flowing air encounters rising elevations, it cools, which causes condensation, a stage that precedes precipitation and cloud development.** In interpreting this diagram, follow the arrows. The diagram depicts air flowing toward hills or mountains. As it does so, the air cools and condensation happens. Based on the arrows, that stage happens before the stages of precipitation and cloud formation. Choice (B) suggests that the air becomes static at the highest elevations, which is not supported by the diagram. Choice (C) also contradicts the diagram. Choice (D) is unsupported because the diagram does not have an east-west orientation: just because the air is depicted flowing from the left-hand side of the picture does not mean that it's flowing from the west.

Lesson 2: Use the Scientific Method

Practice 2, page 29

1.

Independent variable	Dependent variable
combinations of bacteria	acne symptoms

The researchers were studying the question of how different combinations of bacteria affect acne symptoms. Because the researchers thought acne symptoms might depend on differences in bacteria, acne was the researchers' dependent variable. Combinations of bacteria are not affected by acne symptoms, but the researchers thought bacteria might affect those acne symptoms. Therefore, combinations of bacteria were the researchers' independent variable.

2. **B. Different kinds of bacteria may impact acne differently.** The last sentence of the first paragraph provides this answer as well. The researchers "began to wonder whether different strains of bacteria might impact acne in different ways": that statement represents the idea they sought to test—that is, their hypothesis. Choice (A) describes an assumption that was widely held before the researchers began their study. Choice (C) is a suggestion the researchers made after concluding their study, and choice (D) is their conclusion—not their starting hypothesis.

3. **D. Some combinations of bacteria may actually help ward off acne.** This question asks for the researchers' conclusion—that is, the idea they embraced after concluding their study. That idea is described by choice (D). Choice (A) is an assumption many people held before the research began. Choice (B) is not supported by the passage. Choice (C) is not supported by the passage: after drawing their conclusions, the researchers suggested a way to treat acne in the future, but they did not suggest that current treatments are misguided.

4.

a) Form a hypothesis.	iii. Based on your experience, you make a guess about which of the movements involved in playing softball puts the greatest stress on the knees. You suspect that it may be stopping suddenly after running a short distance.
b) Design a test for your hypothesis.	i. You make a list of each of the movements involved in softball. In the off season (when you are not playing entire games), you plan to perform each movement several times without performing the others.
c) Collect data to test your hypothesis.	iv. After performing each movement in isolation, record how your knee feels. Let your knee recover between tests of each type of movement.
d) Form a conclusion based on the data from your test.	ii. Based on the data you collected in your experiment, you think it is likely that stopping suddenly after running a short distance is indeed the cause of your knee pain.

Lesson 3: Reason with Scientific Information

Practice 3, page 31

1. **C. If both objects were currently sitting still, it would require more effort to push the brick across the floor than it would to push the block of wood across the floor.** According to the passage, a heavier object has more inertia, and the brick is heavier than the block. Therefore, you can conclude that it would be harder to move the brick across the floor. Choice (A), breakage, and choice (D), absorbing water, are not mentioned and are irrelevant to this question. Choice (B) is the opposite of the correct answer.

2. **A. The birds that the brown tree snake eats are the primary predators of spiders on Guam.** The scientist's conclusion is that the brown tree snake is the reason there are so many spiders on Guam. The question asks for a piece of information that makes that conclusion more likely—that is, a choice that makes the scientist's conclusion more reasonable or believable. Choice (A) explains why more brown tree snakes would lead to more spiders. Choices (B) and (D) don't link the spiders and snakes at all. Choice (C) describes a relationship between them, but it suggests that more brown tree snakes would lead to *fewer* spiders.

3. **B. If large areas of ice sheets sit on water, the rising of sea levels may proceed more quickly than had previously been predicted.** The main idea of the passage is that some ice sheets may be sitting on water and that those ice sheets may melt more quickly than ice sheets sitting on rock. The passage also states that melting ice sheets contribute to rising sea levels. Putting those two ideas together, a scientist could predict that ice sheets sitting on water might send more melted water into the oceans than would

ice sheets on rock. Choice (A) expresses the opposite of that idea. Choice (C) introduces a comparison that is not supported by the passage. Choice (D) goes too far by insisting that *all* of the quickly melting ice sheets are sitting on water.

4. **A. Most of the ice sheets sitting on water are covering inland lakes with no access to the ocean.** Choice (A) would make the prediction less likely, because if most ice sheets sitting on water have no way to send water into the ocean, then the link between the ice sheets and rising sea levels would be undermined. Choices (B) and (C) actually make the scientist's prediction more likely. Choice (D) may seem to undermine the information in the passage—until you notice that choice (D) criticizes the use of "radar alone" to assess ice sheets. The passage indicates that researchers used both satellite and radar data, which makes choice (D) irrelevant to the prediction.

Lesson 4: Express and Apply Scientific Information

Practice 4, page 33

1. **C. pure acetone; a solution of sugar in acetone** The passage states that, during osmosis, a liquid moves from a place where there is a higher concentration of dissolved material to where there is a lower concentration of dissolved material. Thus, to test the rate of osmosis of a liquid, Gillian would want to put that same liquid on two sides of the vat, with more dissolved material on one side than on the other. Only choice (C) describes that arrangement.

2. **D. formic acid** The solvent with the highest rate of diffusion would be the solvent that took the least time to reach equilibrium. Here it took formic acid the least time to do so.

3. **19.5 minutes** To find the average time, add the times of the

solvents, then divide by the number of solvents.
$$\frac{20 + 25 + 18 + 15}{4} = \frac{78}{4} = 19.5$$

4. **greater than** The passage explains that drinking seawater will result in a higher-than-normal concentration of dissolved material in your bloodstream. Then, according to the passage, water will flow from your tissues into your blood. For that to be an example of osmosis, it must be the case that the water is flowing from a place (your tissues) where the concentration of dissolved material is lower to a place (your blood vessels) where it is higher. Thus, your tissues would start to dry out when the amount of dissolved material in your blood vessels is greater than that in your tissues.

Lesson 5: Use Statistics and Probability

Practice 5, page 35

1. **rabbit** The median is the middle number of a set of numbers, and in this graph, the rabbit has a lower body weight than the dog, human, and horse and a higher body weight than the shrew, cactus mouse, and flying squirrel. It isn't necessary to know the animals' actual body weights to determine this.

2. **rabbit** Similarly, the graph shows that the rabbit has the middle metabolic rate of the seven species in the graph.

3. **lower than the previous average** To find an average, you add up all the numbers in a list and divide by the number of items in the list, like this:

$$\frac{shrew + c.mouse + f.squirrel + rabbit + dog + human + horse}{7}$$

Now, the shrew is the highest of those numbers: it has the highest metabolic rate. Therefore, if you removed it and recalculated the average, the new average would be lower than the previous average.

4. **C. Their metabolic rate would be slightly lower than that of horses.** The question states that elephants weigh more than

horses. Thus, elephants would be to the right of horses on the line graph. Based on the curve of the line, you can guess that elephants would have a slightly lower metabolism than that of horses. Because the line continues to decrease slightly, choice (B) is unsupported.

5. **C. 120** The question asks how many different orderings, or sequences, of the five crops are possible. This is a permutations question, because order matters. Thus, multiply to find the number of permutations:
$5 \times 4 \times 3 \times 2 \times 1 = 120$

Lesson 6: Construct Short Answer Responses

Practice 6, page 37

1. **Short Answer Practice: Explanation**

   Moon Formation Writing Prompt

   3 points maximum

   Read your response and rate it as 3, 2, 1, or 0 based on these criteria:

   3—clear and well-developed explanation; complete support from two or more specific details in passage and/or graphics

   2—partially articulated explanation; partial support from passage and/or graphic

   1—minimal or implied explanation; minimal support from passage and/or graphic

   0—no explanation or support from the passage and/or graphic

   My score: _____

2. **Short Answer Practice: Experiment**

   Caffeine and Blood Components Writing Prompt

   3 points maximum

   Read your response and rate it as 3, 2, 1, or 0 based on these criteria:

   3—well formulated, complete controlled experiment design, hypothesis, data collection method, and criteria for evaluating the hypothesis

   2—logical controlled experimental design, hypothesis, data col-

lection method, and criteria for evaluating the hypothesis

   1—a minimal experimental design, hypothesis, data collection method, and criteria for evaluating the hypothesis

   0—an illogical or no experimental design, hypothesis, data collection method, or criteria for evaluating the hypothesis

   My score: _____

Science Practices Practice Questions, pages 38–41

1. **B. While Copernicus's theory was an important development, it included elements that are outdated today.** The first sentence of the second paragraph provides the main idea. The words "[f]or example" help to make clear that the second and third sentences are details supporting that main idea.

2. **C. The Significance and Limitations of the Copernican Theory** The title of a passage should reflect its topic or main idea. The topic of this passage is the importance, or significance, of Copernicus's theory, as well as the fact that Copernicus's theory was not completely correct. Choices (A) and (D) are both too broad, while choice (B) is incorrect because the passage is not about Copernicus's life.

3. **A. Astronomers now believe that the planets are not embedded in crystalline spheres.** The question asks for something that can be inferred, or deduced, from the passage. Choice (A) is supported by the passage. Copernicus's idea that the planets are embedded in crystalline spheres is mentioned in the second paragraph as an example of an idea that is today considered "primitive." This implies that astronomers today no longer believe this to be true. Choices (B) and (C) are contradicted by the passage. Choice (D) is not supported by the passage: primitive astronomers who came before Copernicus are not discussed.

4. **C. B and D** The passage describes what happens when you add heat to a substance: the

temperature of the substance increases, up to the point when the substance starts to change from a solid to a liquid or from a liquid to a gas. Then the temperature of the substance holds steady while the substance is undergoing that change. When more heat is added but the temperature of a substance remains constant, it must be undergoing a phase change. The places in the diagram where the temperature is flat—B and D—thus represent the two places where the substance is changing from solid to liquid or from liquid to gas.

5. For this question, read the passage carefully to find each type of cancer and identify the cause associated with it.

Type of Cancer	Cause
mesothelioma	long-term asbestos exposure
cervical cancer	human papillomavirus
liver cancer	hepatitis B
lung cancer	long-term regular inhalation of tobacco smoke

6. **B. Penrith** The black bars on the graph represent each city's previous record, and the gray bars represent its current record. Find the city for which the gray bar is furthest above the black bar: Penrith.

7. **C. Penrith** The median number is the middle of a list of numbers. Here, because there are seven cities, the city with the "previous record equal to the median of all the cities' previous records" simply means the city with the middle value (among the previous record values). Fortunately, the cities are represented in the graph in such a way that their previous records are in ascending order, and the median previous record belongs to Penrith.

8. **B. Temperatures increased 5 degrees or less** The largest increase was in the city of Penrith and was approximately 5 degrees.

9. **C. Why, when I touch the metal filing cabinet, do I experience**

more electrostatic shocks than my assistant does when she touches it? The first paragraph of the passage explains that the office manager "wondered why" she experienced more static shocks than her assistant. That's the question that prompted her experiment. While it is true that the office manager decided to switch to cotton clothing, she didn't begin by wondering whether it was better, so choice (A) is incorrect. Choice (B) distorts the office manager's thoughts. Choice (D) places too much emphasis on shoes, which were not the subject of the office manager's experiment.

10. **D. The office manager wore one type of clothing, while her assistant wore another type of clothing, and they recorded the number of shocks they experienced.** The office manager wanted to test her hypothesis that her nylon clothing was causing her to experience shocks when touching a metal filing cabinet. To do so, she conducted an experiment in which she wore cotton clothing for a week, while her assistant wore nylon clothing; both wore identical shoes. Then the manager and assistant recorded the number of shocks they each experienced during the course of a week. Choice (D) correctly describes this experiment. Choice (A) describes the office manager's hypothesis. Choice (B) describes the office manager's course of action after she had completed her experiment, while choice (C) is the opposite of what actually occurred during the experiment (both the manager and the assistant wore identical shoes).

11. **A. They wanted to test the effects of their clothing on the number of shocks they were experiencing, and wearing different types of shoes might have confused their results.** In an experiment, it is important to control factors other than the one thing the experimenter wants to study. In this case, the office manager wanted to study the effect of clothing on

the number of static shocks she was receiving. Choices (B) and (C) wrongly suggest that shoes were the subject of the office manager's experiment. Choice (D) distorts the passage: during her experiment, the office manager was trying to study static shocks—not avoid them.

12. **C. a new hypothesis** Remember, a hypothesis is a guess that a researcher starts with and then tests through an experiment. If the office manager formed a new guess about what was causing the static shocks, and she intended to study that new guess through an experiment, that would be a new hypothesis. It would not, at that point, be choice (A), a new conclusion based on findings. While she might, as choice (D) suggests, design an experiment to test this idea, the idea itself is not an experiment design. And the idea is certainly not choice (B), a general principle from the study of physics; rather, the office manager is making a guess based on observation.

13. **C. 15** This is a combinations question: you are asked for all possible groupings of two out of the six snails, and the order of snails within each group does not matter. Use a table or an organized list to find the number of possible groupings. Name the snails A–F if that makes it easier.

AB				
AC	BC			
AD	BD	CD		
AE	BE	CE	DE	
AF	BF	CF	DF	EF

Count the possible pairs: there are 15.

14. **6.3%** The question asks for the probability that any given star is a class G star, and we have to combine two probabilities to find it. We know that there is a 90 percent chance, or a .9 probability, that a star will be a main sequence star. We also know that, if it is a main sequence star, there is a 7 percent chance, or a .07

probability, that it will be a class G star. Multiply those two probabilities to find the probability of *both* of them happening: $.9 \times .07 = .063$. Express your answer as a percentage: 6.3%.

15. **Science Short Answer Practice: Explanation**
    Swedish Men and Smoking Writing Prompt
    3 points maximum

    Read your response and rate it as 3, 2, 1, or 0 based on these criteria:

    3—**clear and well-developed explanation; complete support** from two or more specific details in passage and/or graphics

    2—**partially articulated explanation; partial support** from passage and/or graphic

    1—**minimal or implied explanation; minimal support** from passage and/or graphic

    0—**no explanation or support** from the passage and/or graphic

    My score: _____

Life Science
Lesson 1: Cell Structures and Functions

Practice 1, page 43

1. **mitochondrion** According to the diagram's labels, energy is produced in the cell's mitochondria (plural of *mitochondrion*).

2. **D. Cell walls cannot maintain a plant's shape and rigidity when the plant lacks water.** Even though cell walls contribute to keeping a plant firm and rigid, they cannot do the job without water-filled vacuoles. This conclusion follows from the fact that a plant that lacks water will wilt.

3. **A. the presence of a nucleus** According to the passage, the presence of a cell nucleus defines a cell as eukaryotic.

4. **A. Each time the microscope is improved, scientists can see cell structures more clearly.** Since cell structures are tiny, the more a cell is magnified, the more detail can be seen.

5. **B. Oxygen would diffuse from the unicellular organism into the pond water.** Since diffusion is the movement of molecules toward areas of lower concentration, if the organism had more oxygen than the surrounding water did, oxygen would pass out of the organism into the water until the concentrations were equalized.

Lesson 2: Cell Processes and Energy

Practice 2, page 45

1. **D. carbon dioxide, water, and energy** According to the equation that summarizes cellular respiration, the products of this process are carbon dioxide, water, and energy.
2. **A. increasing the amount of light the plants receive each day** Because light is required for photosynthesis, increasing light is the best choice for increasing the rate of photosynthesis. The other options either would have no effect or would decrease the rate of photosynthesis.
3. **B. increasing the number of green plants** Because green plants use up carbon dioxide during photosynthesis, increasing the amount of greenery on Earth would help reduce the amount of carbon dioxide in the atmosphere.
4. **stoma** According to the diagram, carbon dioxide enters the leaf through openings in the bottom, called stomata (plural form of *stoma*).
5. **B. Most of a leaf's chloroplasts are found in its palisade cells.** The diagram shows that most of the leaf's chloroplasts are in the palisade cells. Evidence to support the other choices cannot be found in the diagram.

Lesson 3: Human Body Systems

Practice 3, page 47

1. **A. the circulatory system** According to the passage on page 46, the circulatory system transports blood to all the cells of the body.
2. **C. Both are structures in which substances pass through capillary walls into the blood.** Both alveoli and villi are tiny structures containing capillaries in which substances pass to and/or from the blood. In the alveoli of the respiratory system, oxygen and carbon dioxide pass into and out of blood; in the villi of the digestive system, nutrients pass into the blood.
3. **D. Veins have valves that allow blood to flow in one direction only.** Of the four facts given, this is the only one that involves the direction of flow of the blood. Therefore, it helps to support Harvey's conclusion that blood in the veins flows toward the heart.
4. **Ureters** According to the diagram, the ureters are the only structure connecting the kidney to the bladder, so urine must flow through them to reach the bladder.
5. **B. a patient with a painful kidney stone** Because a kidney stone forms in the urinary system, the patient is most likely to be treated by an urologist.

Lesson 4: Health Issues

Practice 4, page 49

1. **D. the skin** As implied by the passage, the skin is one of the first defenses against germs, along with mucous membranes, tears, and stomach acid.
2. **C. habituation** Although Sara feels an urge to drink wine, she feels no ill effects if she does not; this indicates that she is habituated to alcohol. She has a psychological dependence rather than a physical dependence on alcohol. If her dependence were physical, she would feel the effects of skipping her daily drink.
3. **A. Fats are a more concentrated source of energy than carbohydrates.** According to the table, carbohydrates provide 4 calories per gram while fats provide 9 calories per gram. None of the other statements is supported by the information in the table.
4. **B. Carbohydrates come from fruits as well as from bread and rice.** According to the table, bread and rice are not the only foods that provide carbohydrates; fruits and at least one type of vegetable (potatoes) also do. Choices (A) and (D) are recommendations, not facts. Choice (C) is contradicted by the table.

Lesson 5: Reproduction and Heredity

Practice 5, page 51

1. **tall** According to the Punnett square, each parent has the same genotype: Tt. The capital letter *T* represents the tallness allele, and the lowercase *t*, the shortness allele. Because tallness is dominant, each parent plant is tall. The paragraph also states that the parent plants are tall.
2. **B. 1 out of 4** According to the Punnett square, only one out of four possible combinations yields a short plant (one with two recessive alleles for height: tt).
3. **D. TT** If you want to grow only tall plants, then it is better to use purebred tall plants (TT). If you use hybrid tall plants—(Tt) or (tT)—then in the next generation, you will likely get some short plants in your garden.
4. **2** According to the passage on page 50, in order to show a recessive trait, an organism must inherit two recessive alleles for that trait. If it inherits only one recessive allele, the dominant form of the trait will show.
5. **D. Organisms that reproduce sexually produce offspring that have inherited a mix of traits from their parents.** Because they are inheriting a mix of genes from two parents, the offspring of organisms that reproduce sexually are different from the parents and from each other, creating a more diverse population. When an organism reproduces asexually, the offspring are identical to the parent and to each other, which means less diversity in the population.
6. **B. The black male was actually a hybrid.** The only way a white rabbit and a black rabbit could produce a white offspring is if the black rabbit is carrying the recessive allele for white fur. That means the black rabbit was actually a hybrid, not purebred as the student had assumed.

Lesson 6: Modern Genetics

Practice 6, page 53

1. **C. the sequence of base pairs in a gene** According to the third paragraph of the passage on page 52, particular sequences of base pairs code for particular amino acids, which are the building blocks of proteins. Therefore, as the paragraph concludes, the order of bases on a gene forms a code for making a particular protein.
2. **D. a change in protein synthesis** Since DNA provides the blueprint for protein synthesis, any change in DNA may affect protein synthesis.
3. **D. Genetically engineered foods are safe for consumers and the environment.** This is an opinion; it is not a fact that can be proved true from the information in the text. All the other statements are facts, based on information given in the paragraph.
4. **B. so that each daughter cell receives a complete set of DNA** Cell division produces two daughter cells with genetic material, or DNA, that is identical to that of the parent cell. The DNA must be replicated in the parent cell first so that each daughter cell can receive an exact copy of it.
5. **B. The base guanine pairs only with the base cytosine.** According to both the diagram and the passage, in DNA sequences, the base guanine always pairs with the base cytosine. (Note that in the diagram, each base is represented by its initial.) The remaining statements are not supported by the passage or the diagram.
6. **amino acids** Amino acids are described as protein building blocks in the third paragraph of the passage on page 52.

Lesson 7: Evolution and Natural Selection

Practice 7, page 55

1. **B. Frogs' forelimbs contain carpal bones.** All four homologous structures in the diagram include the same layout of bones: humerus, radius, ulna, and carpal bones. Since frogs' limbs are homologous to those of the other three animals, they will likely have the same bones. Choices (A), (C), and (D) may be true, but they are not supported by the diagram.
2. **C. In penguins, flying birds, humans, and alligators, the forelimbs have similar structures despite performing different functions.** Even though the forelimbs of these organisms look alike, they all perform different functions. The arm helps to lift and hold things, the penguin's flipper helps it to swim, the bird's wing helps it to fly, and the alligator's foreleg helps it to walk.
3. **A. traits that make an organism better able to survive in its environment** According to the passage on page 54, adaptations are traits that some individuals possess that enable them to compete successfully in their environment.
4. **C. DNA analysis provides more objective data than observation does.** DNA analysis is more objective than observation, because the person doing the observing must interpret what he or she sees.

Lesson 8: Organization of Ecosystems

Practice 8, page 57

1. **D. the sun** The ultimate source of energy for the food web on the previous page is the sun. This is implied by the first paragraph, which explains that the green plants at the bottom of the food web produce their own energy from the sun. The other species in the food web ultimately depend on those consumers for food.
2. **B. The populations of hares and seed-eating birds would increase.** With fewer foxes to hunt them, more hares and seed-eating birds would survive long enough to reproduce, increasing the populations of these organisms.
3. **B. an aquarium with aquatic plants and herbivorous tropical fish** An aquarium is a human-made ecosystem with living organisms in balance with one another and with their physical environment. It includes both producers (the aquatic plants) and consumers (the herbivorous, which means plant-eating, fish).
4. **D. The natural replacement of lichens by mosses and ferns, and then shrubs, is an example of succession.** According to the information, succession is a naturally occurring replacement of one ecosystem by another.
5. **C. to turn atmospheric nitrogen into compounds plants and animals can use** According to the information, nitrogen-fixing bacteria on the roots of plants like peas and beans take nitrogen and use it to form compounds that plants and animals can use.

Life Science Practice Questions pages 58–61

1. **B. Active transport requires the cell to use energy, and passive transport does not.** According to the information given, the key difference between active and passive transport is the use of the cell's energy.
2. **C. The water level in the jar might have gone down because of evaporation.** Because the experiment did not control for evaporation, it does not prove that the water was absorbed by the ivy.
3.

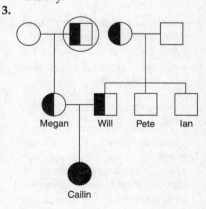

The paragraph indicates that squares stand for males and

half-shading represents genetic carriers. Of all the choices, only the square that represents Megan's father is half-shaded, indicating that Megan's father is a carrier of cystic fibrosis.

4. **D. No one in either Megan's or Will's immediate family has cystic fibrosis except Cailin.** Since everyone in the pedigree except for Cailin has only the recessive gene for cystic fibrosis, no one else suffers from the disease. Thus, Cailin's family members were probably unaware that some of them were carriers for cystic fibrosis.

5. **B. metaphase** According to the diagram, the chromosomes line up across the middle of the cell during metaphase.

6. **B. After mitosis, the two daughter cells have their own nuclei.** The two daughter cells in the interphase section of the diagram each have their own nuclei.

7. **Science Short Answer Practice: Explanation**

   Spindle Fibers Writing Prompt

   3 points maximum

   Read and rate your response as 3, 2, 1, or 0 based on these criteria:

   3—clear and well-developed explanation; complete support from two or more specific details in passage and/or graphics

   2—partially articulated explanation; partial support from passage and/or graphic

   1—minimal or implied explanation; minimal support from passage and/or graphic

   0—no explanation or support from the passage and/or graphic

   My score: _____

8. **C. The fossil record for any given species may be incomplete.** Because fossils are found at random, scientists cannot be sure they have a complete fossil record for many species. An incomplete fossil record would also explain why evolution sometimes seems to take place in bursts rather than gradually.

9. **D. nutrient transport and immune defense** According to the information, plasma transports nutrients. White blood cells defend against infection.

10. **A. enamel** The diagram shows that the top surface of the tooth is made of enamel.

11. **few or no nerve endings** The diagram shows that decay must pass through dentin to reach the pulp. It suggests that decay is only painful once it reaches the pulp due to the many nerve endings located there. Thus, it is likely that the dentin has few or no nerve endings.

12. **B. grazing too many cattle on grassland** Overgrazing of domestic animals like cattle can destroy much plant life in grassland ecosystems. When that happens, the number of cattle the grassland can support decreases, as described in the paragraph.

13. **A. DNA analysis provides more fundamental, accurate data than does a visual analysis of structures and fossils.** Because DNA analysis involves genetic data at the molecular level, it is a better indicator of the relationships among organisms than visible similarities such as teeth. Thus DNA analysis has changed the way scientists previously classified some organisms.

14. **A. panting** A dog's panting and a human being's sweating are both processes that cause loss of body heat through the evaporation of water. In other words, they are body processes that function to cool off an overheated animal.

15. **3** Unintentional injuries, chronic lung diseases, and cancers all caused more deaths in 2011 than in 2005.

16. **biggest decrease** The gray bar representing 2011 is shorter than the black bar representing 2005, meaning the number of deaths decreased. The decrease is greater than that of cerebrovascular disease, and the other three causes of death all increased.

17. **B. 8% decrease** To find the percent change, first subtract to find the amount of the change. The number of deaths from heart diseases in 2005 was roughly 650,000, and the number in 2011 was roughly 600,000. So the amount of change was 50,000. Now, divide that by the original value: $\frac{50,000}{650,000} \approx .08$. To convert that number to a percent, multiply by 100: 8%. Since the number of deaths from heart diseases in 2011 was lower than in 2005, there was an 8 percent decrease.

Earth and Space Science

Lesson 1: Structure of Earth

Practice 1, page 63

1. **A. changes in Earth's crust** According to the passage on page 62, the theory of plate tectonics explains how major landforms are created, the continents move, and the seafloor spreads, all of which are changes in Earth's crust.

2. **(1) consist primarily of iron, (2) is mostly solid, (3) is mostly liquid** As the passage states, both the inner and outer core are made mostly of iron; the main difference is that the outer core is liquid and the inner core is solid.

3. **D. a destructive margin** According to the passage, destructive margins are places where one plate is being forced beneath another, and deep ocean trenches are characteristic of destructive margins between oceanic and continental plates.

4. **D. The west coast of Africa seems to fit into the east coast of the Americas.** Of the four choices, only this one provides evidence to support the idea that there used to be one continent made up of the pieces that are the continents we know today. The fact that two continents seem to fit together like the pieces of a jigsaw puzzle suggests that they were once part of one continent.

5. **C. The continents of North America and Europe are**

moving apart. Since the Atlantic Ocean is getting wider, it follows that the continents on either side of the Atlantic are moving further apart.

6. **B. A single large landmass called Pangaea existed about 250 million years ago.** The existence of Pangaea is a theory based on evidence, not a fact. All the other choices are facts that can be proved true.

Lesson 2: Earth's Resources
Practice 2, page 65

1. **D. 177** To find the consumption of petroleum in 2011, locate 2011 on the horizontal axis. Then imagine a straight vertical line from 2011 to the graph line. Now imagine a straight horizontal line from that spot on the trend line to the vertical axis to find the approximate number of Btus. Note that Btus are British thermal units, a unit for measuring energy.

2. **14** The range of a data set is the difference between its highest value and its lowest value. In 2011, the world petroleum consumption was approximately 177 quadrillion Btus, and in 2003 it was approximately 163 quadrillion Btus. The difference between them is roughly 14 quadrillion Btus.

3. **A. World petroleum consumption increased by about 14 quadrillion Btus between 2003 and 2011.** This is the best summary of the graph because it includes the topic of the graph (world petroleum consumption) and the amount by which consumption changed during the period shown.

4. **D. Waste not, want not.** One of the basic approaches of conservationists is to reduce consumption of resources by decreasing waste ("waste not"). If that is done, in the future the resources will still be available ("want not").

5. **B. Developed nations have started using water more efficiently than they did in the past.** Since population and economic activity are increasing faster than water use in the developed nations, the most likely reason is that people have learned to conserve water, meaning they use water more efficiently now.

6. **D. Soil erosion is caused by both natural forces and the actions of people.** The first sentence mentions several causes of soil erosion. These include natural actions, such as wind, water, and ice, along with human actions, such as deforestation and poor farming practices.

Lesson 3: Weather and Climate
Practice 3, page 67

1. **D. southwest to northeast** The label describes the winds as "westerlies," and the arrows indicate that the winds generally move from the southwest to the northeast. It follows that weather patterns move along with the winds, from southwest to northeast.

2. **B. The winds in the Northern Hemisphere are a mirror image of those in the Southern Hemisphere.** If you compare the two sets of winds, you will see that those in the Northern Hemisphere are a reflection of those in the Southern Hemisphere, just as an image is reflected in a mirror.

3. **D. satellites, which transmit cloud photos and weather data** Satellite photos of cloud patterns help meteorologists identify hurricanes and follow their paths; weather data help them follow changes in the intensity of the storm. Thus, the photos and data from satellites help meteorologists make predictions about the development and movement of hurricanes.

4. **D. global wind and ocean current patterns** According to the passage, both global wind patterns and ocean currents redistribute heat from the solar heating of Earth.

5. **D. The highest temperatures in the atmosphere are in the thermosphere.** According to the chart, the thermosphere has temperatures of up to several thou-sand degrees Fahrenheit—much higher than temperatures in the other layers.

6. **Place your stick figure in the troposphere.** As the lowest layer of the atmosphere, the troposphere is where human beings live and work. Even many airplane flights stay within the troposphere.

Lesson 4: Earth in the Solar System
Practice 4, page 69

1. **D. Mercury** A planet's revolution is its orbit around the sun. Locate the column that shows the planets' revolution periods. Then review the data in the column until you find the shortest revolution period. That would be 88 Earth days, which is the time it takes Mercury to travel once around the sun.

2. **B. Venus** Of all the planets, Venus is closest in size to Earth. Venus's year is also closest in length to Earth's year. These features make Earth and Venus the most similar of the choices given.

3. **C. Uranus was not clearly visible with the telescopes generally in use at the time.** According to the information given, Herschel made excellent, powerful telescopes, so he probably saw a much sharper image of Uranus than did previous astronomers and was therefore able to recognize its unique color and shape.

4. **B. Saturn** Saturn has 53 moons according to the chart. That is many more than Uranus and Neptune, and three more than Jupiter.

5. **D. faith in human judgment and decision-making skills** This is the only value that relates to the possible benefits of sending a crewed mission rather than a robotic mission.

6. **B. an atom, with a dense nucleus and electrons orbiting the nucleus** Of all these choices, the structure of the atom is most similar to the structure of the solar system, even though the atom is much tinier.

Lesson 5: The Expanding Universe

Practice 5, page 71

1. **(1) Sirius; (2) Canopus** The brightest star as seen from Earth is the one with the lowest apparent magnitude. According to the chart, that is Sirius. Absolute magnitude is the measure of brightness of a star as if it were 32.6 light-years away from Earth. Therefore, the star with the lowest absolute magnitude would be the brightest, if all were seen at 32.6 light-years' distance. Canopus has the lowest absolute magnitude, so it is the brightest of the stars.

2. **C. The star's apparent magnitude would be equal to its absolute magnitude.** Since the absolute magnitude of a star is defined as the brightness an object would have at 32.6 light-years from Earth and the apparent magnitude is its brightness as seen from Earth, then an object that was actually 32.6 light-years from Earth would have the same apparent and absolute magnitude.

3. **D. Not all stars are located about 32.6 light-years from Earth.** The apparent magnitude is a measure of how bright the star looks from Earth. (A small, close star might look very bright compared to a large, distant star.) However, the absolute magnitude is a measure of how bright a star would be if it were a set distance from Earth. These numbers are not necessarily similar, since the apparent magnitude does not take the star's distance into account while the absolute magnitude does.

4. **B. It is a main-sequence star.** According to the passage on page 70, stars like the sun have about a 10-billion-year life cycle. Since the main-sequence stage is the longest, a star that is about 4.7 billion years old would be a main-sequence star, in the middle of its life cycle.

5. **D. Pluto should be classified as a dwarf planet.** Choices (A), (B), and (C) are factual details about Pluto. Choice (D) is not a fact but rather a recommendation (that is, an opinion) of the scientists.

Earth and Space Science Practice Questions, page 72–75

1. **A. The moon and the sun exert the greatest pull on Earth's oceans when these bodies are all in a line.** According to the paragraph, when the sun, moon, and Earth are in a line, the highest tides, called spring tides, occur. The paragraph also states that tides are caused by the gravitational pull of the moon and the sun on the oceans. Putting this information together, the paragraph supports the idea that the moon and the sun exert their greatest pull on the oceans when these bodies are all in a line, during spring tides. None of the other statements is supported by the paragraph.

2. **C. Iceland, an island nation in the Atlantic with active volcanoes** An area with active volcanoes has lots of magma near the surface, so it is ideal for geothermal energy, which is a renewable resource.

3. **D. 26 percent** According to the passage, dark matter is matter that does not interact with light, and according to the graph, dark matter may make up 26 percent of the universe.

4. **D. Ordinary matter is made of the chemical elements.** Of all the statements, only choice (D) is a fact that can be proved at this time. The other three choices are hypotheses, proposed explanations for things that have been observed but not proved.

5. **D. tropical-subtropical** First locate the equator on the map. Then consult the map key to identify the climate represented by the most common color that occurs near the equator.

6. **A. The continent with the least area of desert-steppe climate is Europe.** To find the answer to this question, you must check each statement against the map. If the map proves the statement is false, you can eliminate that statement. If the map doesn't show what the statement indicates, you can also eliminate that statement. Choice (A) is the only statement confirmed by the map.

7. **farm output** With a large food output, an area can easily support its human population. This not only contributes to the area's wealth, but it also frees a good portion of the population to do other work, producing wealth.

8. **4** Count the number of climate zones represented on each continent:
North America: 5
South America: 5
Europe: 2 (note the islands near Europe that have a polar climate)
Asia: 5
Australia: 3
Africa: 4
Find the average of those numbers: $\frac{5+5+2+5+3+4}{6}=4$.

9. **(1) Earth; (2) the moon** According to the diagrams, a lunar eclipse occurs when the shadow (the umbra) of Earth falls on the moon, which happens when Earth is between the sun and moon.

10. **C. A lunar eclipse can be seen only at night, and a solar eclipse can be seen only during the day.** The lunar eclipse diagram indicates that a person on the daylight side of Earth would not be able to see the lunar eclipse; only a person on the nighttime side would see it. The solar eclipse diagram indicates that a person on the nighttime side of Earth would not be able to see the eclipse; only a person on the daytime side would see it.

11. **D. a catalytic converter, a device in the exhaust system of a vehicle that reduces harmful emissions from the engine** Of all the choices, only this one reduces the harmful pollutants of burning fossil fuel and so would reduce acid rain.

12. **Science Short Answer Practice: Explanation**

Acid Rain Writing Prompt

3 points maximum

Read your response and rate it as 3, 2, 1, or 0 based on these criteria:

3—clear and well-developed explanation; complete support from two or more specific details in passage and/or graphics

2—partially articulated explanation; partial support from passage and/or graphic

1—minimal or implied explanation; minimal support from passage and/or graphic

0—no explanation or support from the passage and/or graphic

My score: _____

13. **A. The rock cycle is a continuous process of rock formation, destruction, and reformation.** The diagram is a cycle diagram, which shows a process that occurs again and again; in this case, the process of the formation and destruction of rocks.

14. **sedimentary rock** An imprint can only occur in soft material like sand, mud, or silt. The diagram shows that when this material is compacted, sedimentary rock forms. This rock will contain the imprint as a fossil. Note that fossils sometimes also occur in metamorphic rock, but this is not presented as an option.

15. **A. melted rock** According to the diagram, igneous, sedimentary, and metamorphic rocks all form magma by melting.

16. **C. Open-pit mining destroys valuable land.** An open-pit mine destroys a huge area, so it is restricted in many countries to prevent large-scale destruction of land. There is no reason to suspect, based on the information given, that choice (B), open-pit mining, is more dangerous than shaft mining or choice (D)—it yields lower-grade minerals.

Physical Science

Lesson 1: Atoms and Molecules

Practice 1, page 77

1. **A. The sodium atom loses an electron, becoming positively**

charged, and the chlorine atom gains an electron, becoming negatively charged. According to the diagram, the sodium atom gives up an electron to the chlorine atom. With one fewer electron than protons, the sodium becomes a positively charged ion. When the chlorine atom gains an electron, it has one more electron than protons, making it a negatively charged ion. The sodium and chloride ions are attracted to each other, forming an ionic bond.

2. **D. $C_6H_{12}O_6$** According to the passage on page 76 and the question text, a chemical formula represents the number of atoms of each element in a compound. Chemical symbols, which are letters, represent the elements, followed by subscripts, which represent the number of atoms.

3. **(1) not necessarily either positively or negatively charged, (2) either positively or negatively charged** The key difference between a non-ionized atom and an ion is the gain or loss of an electron, which gives the ion either a negative or a positive charge.

4. **B. Most of the alpha particles passed right through the gold foil.** Because most of the alpha particles passed right through the foil without being stopped or deflected, Rutherford concluded that atoms must consist mostly of empty space.

5. **B. 11** The atomic number of sodium refers to how many protons the atom has. An atom that is not an ion has the same number of protons as electrons. Therefore, a sodium atom has 11 electrons.

Lesson 2: Properties and States of Matter

Practice 2, page 79

1. **A. melting and boiling** According to the passage on page 78, adding heat to a solid melts the solid, and adding heat to a liquid causes it to boil, or change to a gas.

2. **B. Solids are usually denser than liquids and gases.** If you

compare the densities of the solids, liquids, and gases in the chart, you will see that the solids are denser than the liquids and the gases.

3. **190** According to the paragraph, glycerin's boiling point is 190° greater than water's boiling point. To find the percentage by which glycerin's boiling point is greater than that of water, divide the difference between the two substances' boiling points by the boiling point of water and multiply the quotient by 100%. Thus, $\frac{190}{100} \times 100\% = 190\%$. Always read questions carefully. Glycerin's boiling point is 290 percent of water's boiling point, but this question asks for the percent by which glycerin's boiling point is *greater than* water's.

4. **A. Water is a unique substance on Earth.** This statement is a conclusion (a general statement) that is supported by the statements that give details about the properties of water.

5. **B. Antifreeze added to water in a car's radiator lowers the freezing point below 0°C.** Adding antifreeze (a solute) to water (a solvent) lowers the freezing point of the solution, the liquid in the radiator.

6. **D. Dusty air** Dusty air is the only choice with large suspended particles. Gold and oxygen are elements, not mixtures. Salt water is a solution; it has small particles that do not settle out of the mixture.

Lesson 3: Chemical Reactions

Practice 3, page 81

1. **C. $2Cu + O_2 \rightarrow 2CuO$** You can eliminate choice (A) because the product (CuO) is on the left side of the equation rather than on the right side. To determine which of the remaining answer choices is correct, you must look for the equation that has two copper atoms and two oxygen atoms on the left side to balance the two copper atoms and two oxygen atoms on the right side.

2. **B. Weigh the reactants, conduct the reaction in a sealed container,**

and weigh the products. This procedure should result in the weights of the reactants and products being equal, because none of the products would escape from the sealed container. The weight measurements would provide evidence for the law of the conservation of mass.

3. **Juanita ignites the gas = activation energy** Activation energy is the amount of energy required to start the reaction. **The gas burns = exothermic energy** Burning gas creates exothermic energy, given off in the form of heat and light. **The egg solidifies = endothermic energy** The energy the reactants absorb from their surroundings is endothermic energy.

4. **C. The time during which the reaction occurs** The horizontal axis is labeled "Time," so you can eliminate choice (D). The graph shows the progress of the reaction, which takes place over time, not just one instant of the reaction, so you can eliminate choices (A) and (B).

5. **A. Compounds are substances consisting of two or more elements chemically combined in a definite proportion.** The writer of the paragraph takes for granted that you know what a compound is and does not define the term *compound* in the paragraph. The other answer choices are stated explicitly in the paragraph.

6. **B. "Acids and Bases"** The passage gives an overview of acids and bases and describes what happens when they react with one another.

Lesson 4: The Nature of Energy

Practice 4, page 83

1. **C. Energy cannot be created or destroyed, but can only change in form.** According to the third paragraph on page 82, this is the law of conservation of energy.

2. **chemical, electrical, light** The batteries use chemical energy and convert it to electrical energy, which is converted to light energy in the filament of the lightbulb.

3. **B. power** Power is the rate at which work is done or, in this case, the rate at which energy is consumed. The wood stove has greater power than the oak tree because it consumes the tree's energy in much less time than it takes the tree to consume the sun's energy.

4. **B. the relationship between energy and mass** According to the passage, Einstein's equation explains how energy can be converted to mass, and vice versa.

5. **B. At the high point of its swing, a pendulum has potential energy.** The diagram shows that at the high point of its swing, the pendulum has potential energy, the energy of position. The information in the diagram does not support any of the other statements.

6. **A. The molecules in air are far apart.** Because the molecules of a gas like air are far apart, they are in contact with one another less frequently than are the molecules of a liquid or solid, since liquids and solids are much denser. That is why gases have lower conductivity than liquids and solids do.

Lesson 5: Motion and Forces

Practice 5, page 85

1. **D. anything that changes the rest or motion of an object** According to the passage on page 84, this is the definition of a force.

2. **D. the tendency of an object to remain at rest or in motion** According to the third paragraph on page 84, inertia is described in Newton's first law of motion as the tendency of objects to remain at rest or keep moving until acted upon by a force.

3. **B. the International Space Station orbiting Earth** The key concept regarding centripetal force is circular motion, and the orbit of the space station is the only example of circular motion among the options given.

4. **the momentum of a car decreases when its velocity decreases** The fifth paragraph on page 84 indicates that momentum

is calculated by multiplying mass and velocity. Slowing a car before a collision decreases the car's momentum. Because momentum is a measure of energy of movement, slowing the cars will result in less energy on collision and so less damage to both cars.

5. **B. an object that has a constant speed** The graph shows a straight line that slopes upward. According to the paragraph, this type of graph shows an object that is moving at a constant speed.

6. **C. Some machines simply change the direction of a force.** According to the information given, a machine is a device that changes the direction *or* the size of a force, which means that some machines change only the direction of the force. An example is a simple pulley, which allows you to push down, rather than pull up, to lift a load.

Lesson 6: Electricity and Magnetism

Practice 6, page 87

1. **B. two poles repelling one another** According to the diagram, like poles repel, so a drawing of two north poles facing each other would look the same as the diagram of two south poles facing each other.

2. **A. Copper and aluminum are conductors.** Electrical wires need to be made of something that carries electricity easily, which is what conductors do.

3. **D. a flashlight** According to the passage, direct current is used in battery-powered devices. Choice (D) is correct because flashlights typically run on batteries.

4. **D. a transformer** According to the passage, transformers change the voltage of an incoming electric current.

5. **lightbulb** According to the paragraph, a device that gets power from a current is called a resistor. Since the battery in the circuit powers the lightbulb, the lightbulb is a resistor.

6. **C. Disconnecting the light bulb will also stop the current.**

To have current, you need to have a loop. Getting rid of any piece of the circuit—the battery, the switch, the lightbulb, or the wire—would break the loop and thus stop the current.

Physical Science Practice Questions pages 88–91

1. **B. 5,730 years** This information is in the table, in the row for carbon-14 and the column for half-life.

2. **D. Uranium produces radioactive waste that may harm living things for millions of years.** Since the question asks what an *opponent* of nuclear power would say, the correct answer should be a negative fact about uranium. According to the table, uranium is unstable for millions or even billions of years, so choice (D) is both negative and true. Choice (C) is a negative claim about uranium, but it's a false one—uranium is unstable for much longer than three days.

3. **D. Both involve the transfer of energy through matter or space.** According to the paragraph, a wave is something that transfers energy through matter or space, so both types of waves would have that in common. Longitudinal waves have forward-and-back displacement, while transverse waves have up-and-down displacement, so choices (A) and (B) are incorrect. Choice (C) is incorrect because only longitudinal waves involve compressions.

4. **A. A cork in water bobs up and down as waves pass.** The question asks for an example in which something stays in roughly the same place after a wave passes through it. If a cork merely bobs up and down as waves pass, then the cork will be in its original position after the waves stop. Thus, choice (A) is the right example.

5. **A. dust motes dancing in a shaft of sunlight** Brownian motion is the random movement of particles in a liquid or a gas. Choice (A) is correct because

dust motes move about randomly in the air, which is a gas. Choice (C) is wrong because it doesn't involve movement, choice (D) is wrong because the raft is *on* a lake (not *in* it), and choice (B) is wrong because the ground is a solid.

6. **Increase rate of reaction: Use powdered marble. Decrease rate of reaction: Use larger chunks of marble.** The passage says that the greater the surface area of the reactants, the faster the reaction will go. *Surface area* in this case refers to the amount of marble in contact with the acid. Thus, using larger chunks of marble will slow down the reaction, since larger chunks will have more "inner" marble, which won't be exposed to the acid. This will reduce the surface area. On the other hand, using powdered marble will mean that practically all of the marble is exposed to the acid, making the surface area large and causing the reaction to go faster.

7. **decreases** The paragraph says that the bigger the pressure, the smaller the volume (and vice versa). So, when pressure increases, volume will decrease.

8. **C. xenon (Xe)** According to the chart, the noble gases are in column 18. Choice (C), xenon, is the only choice in this column.

9. **B. Chlorine (Cl) and iodine (I) have similar properties.** According to the information given, elements in the same column have similar properties. Since chlorine and iodine are in the same column, choice (B) is correct.

10. **A. microwaves** According to the diagram, wavelengths increase as you go left to right. Since microwaves are to the right of the visible spectrum, choice (A) is correct.

11. **C. People can see only a small portion of the electromagnetic spectrum.** In the diagram, the visible spectrum—the section that people can see—is only a small piece of the entire electromagnetic spectrum.

12. **B. Its mass remains the same, and its weight decreases.**

The mass of an object doesn't depend on anything; rather, mass is a property of the object. By contrast, the weight of an object gets smaller as the object gets farther from Earth. So, as a rocket travels away from Earth, its mass won't change, but its weight will get smaller.

13. **B. Coldness cannot be transferred.** The paragraph directly states that heat can be transferred, choice (A), a cold object can be warmed by your body (choice (C)), and that your body heat can be lost (choice (D)). What the passage assumes but doesn't say is that *only* heat can be transferred; coldness can't be. This is choice (B).

14. **D. the range** All of the engineer's recorded speeds are off by 3.7 km/hour, which skews the mean, mode, and median upward. However, the range is unchanged, because the difference between the largest value and the smallest value is the same in both columns (195.6 km/hour).

15. **C. $\frac{3}{5}$** This question asks about the planes' actual speeds, so be sure to use the "actual speed" column. Four of the five planes have a speed less than 360 km/hour, and once one of those planes is chosen, three of the four remaining planes will have a speed less than 360 km/hour. Thus, the probability that both chosen planes have a speed less than 360 km/hour is $\frac{4}{5} \times \frac{3}{4} = \frac{3}{5}$.

16. **Science Short Answer Practice: Experiment Design**

    Decongestant Writing Prompt

    3 points maximum

    Read your response and rate it as 3, 2, 1, or 0 based on these criteria:

    3—**well-formulated,** complete controlled experiment design, hypothesis, data collection method, and criteria for evaluating the hypothesis

2—logical controlled experimental design, hypothesis, data collection method, and criteria for evaluating the hypothesis

1—a minimal experimental design, hypothesis, data collection method, and criteria for evaluating the hypothesis

0—an illogical or no experimental design, hypothesis, data collection method, or criteria for evaluating the hypothesis

My score: _____

Practice Test

1. To practice for the actual GED® Science Test, you can take the following practice test. When you do, follow the same time limits you will face on the actual test.

   - **Science, 32 Questions and 2 Short Answers, $1\frac{1}{2}$ Hours**

   Just as on the actual tests, you will work with a variety of formats:

   - For the **multiple-choice questions**, you may fill in the circles next to the correct answers in this book, or you can write your answers on a separate piece of paper.
   - For **other formats**, directions will indicate where you can write in boxes, on lines, or place a dot on a specific place on a graphic.
   - You can write **short answers** on a computer, or, if one is not available, on a sheet of paper.

   NOTE: Writing your responses on a computer is preferable because you will be composing your responses on a computer when you take the GED® test. However, if you do not have a computer available when you take these tests, write your responses on paper so that you can evaluate your writing samples.

2. **You may use your calculator** as needed during the Science Test.

3. **Check** your answers using the *Practice Test Answers and Explanations* that begin on page 119, and fill in the *Practice Test Evaluation Charts* on page 122. These charts will allow you to see which study areas may still need work.

4. **Confirm** your readiness to take the actual GED® Science Test.

Directions: Use 35 minutes to answer the following 16 questions. You may fill in the circles next to the correct answers or write your answers in boxes or on lines as indicated.

Question 1 refers to the following paragraph and diagram.

Newton's third law of motion states that when one object exerts a force upon another object, the second object exerts an equal force on the first, in the opposite direction. An airplane in motion changes the speed and direction of the air, exerting a force on it. The opposing force of the air keeps the airplane aloft.

How an Airplane Flies

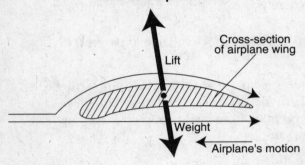

1. What vertical force holds the airplane up?

   ○ A. lift
   ○ B. Newton's third law
   ○ C. weight
   ○ D. air resistance

2. Sleep may have evolved in humans for several reasons. First, people were unable to hunt, gather food, or travel in the dark. Second, sleep provides an opportunity to repair our body's cells, especially those in the brain. Third, our body temperature is lower during sleep, which conserves energy. Fourth, during deep sleep the pituitary gland releases a growth hormone, so sleep may play a role in growth.

   Which of the following is the best title for this paragraph?

   ○ A. "Sleep and Growth"
   ○ B. "Our Brains During Sleep"
   ○ C. "Why We Sleep"
   ○ D. "The Role of Deep Sleep"

3. You MAY use your calculator on this question.

   A scientist shines a laser through six beakers, each containing a different liquid substance, and measures the laser beam's angle of refraction. The scientist records her measurements for liquids A–E in the table below; her measurement for liquid F is lost.

Liquid	Angle of Refraction (degrees)
A	15
B	32
C	12
D	47
E	15
F	?

   However, the scientist recalls that the mean of all six angle measurements was 23 degrees. What must the laser beam's angle of refraction through liquid F have been?

   Write your answer in the box below.

Questions 4 through 6 are based on the following information and graphic.

The processes that circulate nitrogen between the atmosphere, land, and organisms are called the nitrogen cycle.

The Nitrogen Cycle

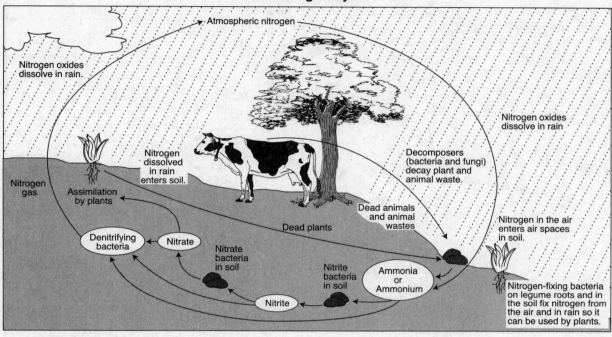

4. Nitrogen-fixing bacteria are found both in the soil and on the roots of legumes like peas and beans. From where do these bacteria get nitrogen?

    ○ A. ammonia and ammonium
    ○ B. the air and rainwater in the soil
    ○ C. animals and animal wastes
    ○ D. animal wastes and decaying plants

5. Which of the following statements is a conclusion about the nitrogen cycle rather than a detail in the diagram?

    ○ A. Nitrogen oxides dissolve in rainwater.
    ○ B. Nitrogen-fixing bacteria are found both in the soil and on the roots of legumes.
    ○ C. The recycling of nitrogen through the biosphere involves many complex processes.
    ○ D. Nitrite bacteria turn ammonia and ammonium into nitrites.

6. To increase the nitrogen content of the soil, many farmers spread synthetic fertilizers containing nitrogen compounds. What might an organic farmer, who does not use synthetic fertilizers, do to improve the fertility of the soil?

    ○ A. switch to crops requiring more potassium
    ○ B. compost with plant and animal wastes
    ○ C. plant more nonleguminous plants
    ○ D. switch to crops requiring more nitrogen

Question 7 refers to the following graph.

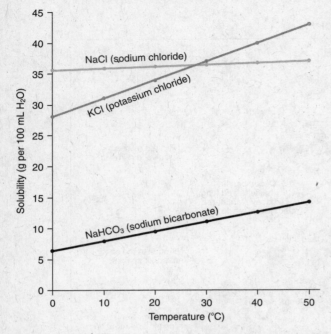

**Solubility of Common Compounds
in Grams of Solute per 100 mL of Water**

7. Which of the following statements is supported by the information in the graph?

○ A. About 15 grams of sodium bicarbonate will dissolve in 100 mL of water at 10°C.
○ B. About 30 grams of potassium chloride will dissolve in 100 mL of water at 30°C.
○ C. Sodium chloride shows the greatest increase in solubility with increase in temperature.
○ D. For the three compounds shown, solubility increases as temperature increases.

8. Directions: Following the scientific method, a researcher conducted an experiment using houseplants. Match each action the scientist took to the step in the scientific method below.

Step of the scientific method	The scientist's action
Step 1. Formulate a question about a phenomenon	
Step 2. Collect data	
Step 3. Form a hypothesis	
Step 4. Test the hypothesis through an experiment	
Step 5. Draw a conclusion	

a.	For 6 weeks, the scientist used water at 75 degrees to water plants in Group A and used water at 55 degrees to water plants in Group B. He recorded their growth during this period.
b.	The scientist wondered whether water at different temperatures might affect houseplants differently.
c.	The scientist researched the growth rate of plants at various greenhouses, some of which use cool water and some of which use warm water to water their plants.
d.	At the end of 6 weeks, the plants in Group A were, on average, 2" taller than plants in Group B. The scientist interpreted this to mean that warm water is better for plants than cool water.
e.	The scientist guessed that warm water might be better for plants than cool water.

9. Atoms are composed of protons (positive charge), neutrons (no charge), and electrons (negative charge). Because an atom has an equal number of protons and electrons, it has a total charge of zero.

What would happen if an atom lost an electron?

○ A. Its charge would become positive.
○ B. Its charge would become negative.
○ C. Its charge would remain neutral.
○ D. Its neutrons would gain a positive charge.

10. Weathering is the breaking down of rock by rain, frost, wind, and other elements. No transport is involved in weathering. The weathered rock remains in place. Weathering can be physical, involving abrasion—the wearing away of a surface—or changes in temperature; it can be chemical, involving chemical reactions; or it can be organic, involving the action of living things.

Which of the following is an example of physical weathering?

○ A. the cracking of granite from the expansion of freezing water
○ B. the breakdown of calcite by reaction with acids in fertilizer
○ C. the transport of sand by the wind
○ D. the breakdown of crumbling rock in the soil by burrowing worms

11. When removed from the body, large organs live only a few hours or days under cold conditions. Therefore, organ transplants must be performed quickly. Many organs go to waste because the organ cannot be transported to an appropriate patient in the short time available. Unfortunately, it is not yet possible to freeze large organs to preserve them for a longer period. That's because they contain many different types of cells, all of which react differently to freezing. Some cells are even destroyed by the ice crystals that form during freezing.

Which of the following studies is most likely to yield information that might help solve the specific problem of freezing whole organs for transplant?

○ A. how the time it takes to locate patients who need organs can be decreased
○ B. how the time it takes to transport organs to their destinations can be decreased
○ C. how special fluids keep insects alive during subfreezing weather
○ D. how radioactive isotopes can be used to diagnose the condition of donated organs

12. Most animals have bodies that exhibit either bilateral symmetry or radial symmetry. If you drew a straight line down the middle of an animal exhibiting bilateral symmetry, the two sides would be mirror images of one another. Such animals have a front end and a rear end. On the other hand, an animal exhibiting radial symmetry has a body consisting of similar parts arranged around a center.

Circle the image of the animal(s) below displaying a radially symmetrical body plan.

A. salt marsh greenhead fly

B. sea star

C. dogfish

D. horseshoe crab

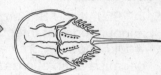

13. Hydrogen peroxide molecules are composed of two hydrogen atoms and two oxygen atoms. Water is also composed of hydrogen and oxygen, but water has one fewer oxygen atom than hydrogen peroxide does. Which of the following statements best describes the chemical reaction shown in the equation below?

$$2H_2O_2 \rightarrow 2H_2O + O_2$$

○ A. Hydrogen peroxide is being made out of water and air.
○ B. Hydrogen peroxide is decomposing into pure water.
○ C. Hydrogen peroxide is decomposing into water and oxygen.
○ D. Water and oxygen are combining to make hydrogen peroxide.

Question 14 refers to the following chart.

Melting and Boiling Points

Element	Melting Point, F	Boiling Point, F
Mercury	−38	675
Bromine	19	138
Iron	2,795	5,184
Carbon	6,420	8,720
Gold	1,945	5,379

14. Which of the following statements is sup-ported by the information in the chart?

   ○ A. Mercury and bromine are liquids at room temperature.

   ○ B. Iron has a higher melting point than carbon.

   ○ C. Iron has a higher boiling point than gold.

   ○ D. Mercury, bromine, iron, carbon, and gold are all metals.

15. In 1969, the U.S. Surgeon General announced that infectious bacterial diseases would soon become a thing of the past because antibiotic drugs had become so effective against them. However, since that time, strains of disease-causing bacteria that are resistant to antibiotics have evolved. Some types of pneumonia and gastrointestinal infections are now untreatable by antibiotics. About 17 million people worldwide still die annually from infectious diseases.

Which of the following best explains why the U.S. Surgeon General's prediction was wrong?

   ○ A. Antibiotic drugs are not effective against most disease-causing bacteria.

   ○ B. Infectious diseases are also caused by viruses and parasites.

   ○ C. Infectious diseases have remained a problem outside the United States.

   ○ D. Bacteria quickly evolved resistance to antibiotic drugs.

16. A student did an experiment to see how far a ball would roll on different surfaces. She made five different ramps, each with a different surface: a plain pine board, a painted board, a board covered with sandpaper, a board covered with artificial turf, and a board covered with shag carpet. She set up his experiment on a smooth, level floor. To make the ramps, she raised one end of each board with a book. She collected four copies of the science textbook her class was using and set up four of the ramps with these books. She couldn't find a fifth copy of the book, so she used a thinner science study guide to set up the fifth ramp. She rolled a tennis ball down each ramp and measured how far the ball traveled each time. Then she compiled his data and drew conclusions.

Why was the student's experiment flawed?

   ○ A. The student should have used a ball with a smooth surface rather than a tennis ball.

   ○ B. The student should have used books of the same height for all of the ramps.

   ○ C. The student should not have used sandpaper as one of the surfaces.

   ○ D. For a control, the student should have rolled the ball across a piece of wood that was level.

Directions: Read the article and respond to the writing prompt below. Type your response on a computer, if one is available. If you do not have access to a computer, write your response neatly on paper. This task may require approximately 10 minutes to complete.

1   A local candy company has had great success with its new neon candy bars. The neon candy bars are featured in a range of five bright colors. They were designed to entice children with their visual appeal and have been selling extremely well since their release.

2   Recently, the company has been flooded with complaints that children are experiencing extreme hyperactivity shortly after consuming the neon candy bars. The company's original candy bars have not generated similar complaints. The only differences between the original candy bars and the new neon candy bars are the neon color of the bar, increased sugar content, and a design change on the outside of the packaging.

3   The candy company's development team has been debating what could be causing the hyperactivity. Developer A suggests that the type of food coloring used in the neon candy bars is causing the hyperactivity and a new type of food coloring should be explored. This claim has a basis in a study conducted a few years earlier that showed a competitor's candy bar increasing hyperactivity when the same food coloring was used.

4   Developer B doesn't believe that the food coloring responsible. She suggests that the increased sugar content of the neon candy bars is to blame for the hyperactivity the children are experiencing. While there is little scientific evidence linking sugar to hyperactivity, many parents of hyperactive children claim that sugar makes their children's behavior problems worse.

5   Developer C believes it is the new ink used on the packaging. On some items, the ink can leak through the thin wrapper and affect the product. The new design incorporates neon colors, and the ink used to produce those colors is made of harsher chemicals than were previously used.

Write a Short Answer Response

As part of an experiment conducted by the candy company, a group of children is given a new candy bar formulated with less sugar than the neon candy bars. This group of children experiences extreme hyperactivity. What could be causing the hyperactivity? Using information from the passage, suggest a hypothesis in answer to this question. Cite specific information from the passage as support for why your suggestion is plausible.

Directions: Use 35 minutes to answer the following 16 questions. You may fill in the circles next to the correct answers or write your answers in boxes or on lines as indicated.

Question 17 refers to the following paragraph and diagram.

Herbivores are animals that eat only plants; carnivores are animals that eat animals. Typical herbivore and carnivore teeth patterns are shown below.

Typical Teeth Patterns in Carnivores and Herbivores

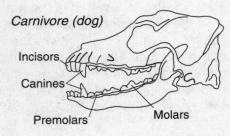

Carnivore (dog)

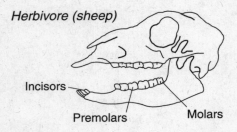

Herbivore (sheep)

17. What is the most notable difference between the dog's teeth and the sheep's teeth?

  ○ A. The dog has fewer teeth than the sheep does.
  ○ B. The dog has molars and the sheep does not.
  ○ C. The dog has incisors and the sheep does not.
  ○ D. The dog has canines and the sheep does not.

Question 18 refers to the following chart.

The Five Largest Asteroids

Name	Average distance from sun (Earth = 1)	Time to orbit sun
Ceres	2.77	4.6 years
Pallas	2.77	4.6 years
Vesta	2.36	3.6 years
Hygeia	3.13	5.5 years
Interamnia	3.06	5.4 years

18. Which of the following statements is supported by the information in the chart?

  ○ A. Pallas is further away from the sun than Hygeia is.
  ○ B. Of the five largest asteroids, Vesta has the longest orbital period.
  ○ C. The five largest asteroids are all farther from the sun than Earth is.
  ○ D. Of the five largest asteroids, only Interamnia takes more than five years to orbit the sun.

19. The American lobster, *Homerus americanus,* is typically bluish-green to brown in coloration. However, a rare genetic mutation, estimated to occur in 1 in 2 million lobsters, can result in a bright blue-colored shell. In 2011, 220 million pounds of lobsters, typically weighing 1–9 pounds each, were caught; two blue lobsters were reported in that time.

In 2011, the experimental probability of catching a blue lobster was [Select...▼] the estimated probability of a lobster having the blue mutation.

- greater than
- approximately the same as
- less than

Question 20 is based on the following diagram.

Structure of a Volcano

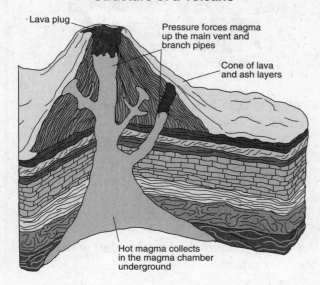

20. Based on the diagram, what causes a volcano to erupt?

- A. Pressure builds up inside the magma chamber and vent.
- B. Magma flows down toward the underground chamber.
- C. The lava plug at the top of the main vent wears away.
- D. The lava plug at the top of the main vent collapses inward.

21. In a chemical reaction, the atoms of the reactants are rearranged to form products with different chemical and physical properties. A catalyst is a substance that speeds the rate at which a chemical reaction takes place. The catalyst itself is unchanged at the end of the reaction. In which of the following reactions is a catalyst at work?

- A. when an acid is neutralized, as when hydrochloric acid is added to sodium hydroxide yielding sodium chloride and water
- B. when food is digested, as when an enzyme in saliva called ptyalin breaks down starch into sugars without itself changing
- C. when copper is oxidized by combining with nitric acid to yield copper nitrate, nitrogen dioxide, and water
- D. when baking soda is heated, causing the sodium bicarbonate to break down, yielding carbon dioxide gas as a byproduct

22. For five years, researchers at the University of Wisconsin Medical School ran an experiment in which they evaluated the hearing of 3,753 people between the ages of 48 and 92. Of the group, 46 percent were nonsmokers, 30.3 percent were former smokers, and 14.7 percent still smoked. The scientists found that smokers were nearly 1.7 times as likely as nonsmokers to suffer hearing loss. The study suggests that age-related hearing loss might be preventable.

Which of the following statements is most likely to have been the researchers' hypothesis?

- A. Smoking has been shown to harm health in many different ways.
- B. People can reduce their chances of developing age-related hearing loss by not smoking.
- C. The University of Wisconsin study group consisted of 3,753 people between the ages of 48 and 92.
- D. Smokers were nearly 1.7 times as likely as nonsmokers to suffer hearing loss.

Question 23 refers to the following graphs.

Elements in Humans and Bacteria

Humans

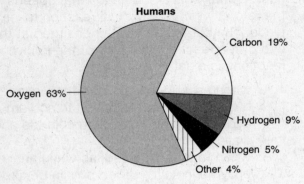

Carbon 19%

Oxygen 63%

Hydrogen 9%

Nitrogen 5%

Other 4%

Bacteria

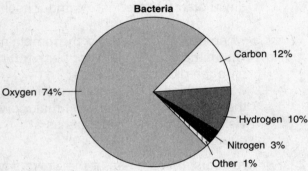

Carbon 12%

Oxygen 74%

Hydrogen 10%

Nitrogen 3%

Other 1%

23. What is one of the main differences between the composition of humans and that of bacteria?

   ○ A. Humans contain elements other than oxygen, carbon, nitrogen, and hydrogen and bacteria do not.

   ○ B. Humans contain a higher percentage of oxygen than bacteria do.

   ○ C. Humans contain a higher percentage of hydrogen than bacteria do.

   ○ D. Humans contain a higher percentage of carbon than bacteria do.

Question 24 refers to the following diagrams.

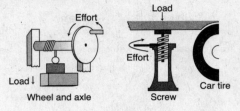

Effort

Load

Load ↓

Effort

Wheel and axle

Screw

Car tire

24. What do the wheel and axle and the screw have in common?

   ○ A. Both increase the effort needed to move a load.

   ○ B. Both involve effort applied with circular motion.

   ○ C. Both involve effort applied with horizontal motion.

   ○ D. Both involve effort applied with vertical motion.

25. During various periods in Earth's history, average global temperatures have dropped, resulting in ice ages. During an ice age, glaciers cover large regions of Earth. Scientists disagree about what causes ice ages. One hypothesis suggests that there have been long term changes in Earth's orbit, causing the planet to periodically move farther from the sun. Another view proposes that a periodic increase in volcanic activity increases the dust in the atmosphere, blocking the sun's rays. Still another hypothesis suggests that changes in Earth's own radiant energy cause ice ages. And finally, other scientists propose that changes in the direction of ocean currents cause ice ages.

Which of the following statements is a fact and NOT an opinion or hypothesis?

   ○ A. During an ice age, temperatures drop and ice covers vast areas of Earth.

   ○ B. Changes in Earth's orbit cause temperature fluctuations and ice ages.

   ○ C. Large amounts of volcanic dust blocking the sun's energy cause ice ages.

   ○ D. Changes in Earth's own radiant energy cause ice ages.

Question 26 refers to the following diagram.

Ether (C_2H_6O)

```
    H       H
    |       |
H — C — O — C — H          Key
    |       |
    H       H              C = Carbon

                           H = Hydrogen
**Ethanol ($C_2H_5OH$)**
                           O = Oxygen
    H   H
    |   |
H — C — C — OH
    |   |
    H   H
```

26. What is the main difference between the hydrocarbons ether and ethanol?

   ○ A. Ether has carbon, hydrogen, and oxygen atoms, and ethanol has only carbon and hydrogen atoms.
   ○ B. Ether has three carbon atoms and ethanol has two carbon atoms.
   ○ C. Ether has one oxygen atom and ethanol has two oxygen atoms.
   ○ D. The arrangement of the carbon, hydrogen, and oxygen atoms in the two hydrocarbons is different.

27. In 1861, Charles Darwin, a naturalist who formulated the theory of evolution, remarked that the science of geology had made much progress in his lifetime. He wrote, "About thirty years ago there was much talk that geologists ought only to observe and not theorize; and I well remember someone saying that at this rate a man might as well go into a gravel-pit and count the pebbles and describe the colors. How odd it is that anyone should not see that all observation must be for or against some view if it is to be of any service!"

Which of the following statements best summarizes Darwin's view of the role of observation in science?

   ○ A. Observation is the best way to gather facts about any aspect of nature.
   ○ B. Observation is useful as long as it is supported by statistics.
   ○ C. Observation should be used only in the field of geology.
   ○ D. Observation is useful as long as the results are used to support or disprove a hypothesis.

28. Directions: Match each process to an example of that process.

The four types of processes that create minerals in Earth's crust are called *magmatic, hydrothermal, metamorphic*, and *surficial*. Magmatic processes involve the heating and cooling of magma deep inside the Earth's mantle to form crystals. Hydrothermal processes are caused by the movement of water within Earth's crust. Metamorphic processes involve combinations of heat, pressure, time, water, and various solutions to change existing mineral deposits and form new ones. Surficial processes are physical processes that affect rock at Earth's surface or in the loose material—soil and dust—that covers Earth's crust.

Type of process	Example of process
Magmatic	
Hydrothermal	
Metamorphic	
Surficial	

a. Wind eroding away the softer components in sandstone
b. A gradual increase in temperature in the mantle, followed by a sudden drop in temperature
c. Movement of seawater through fractured rock underground
d. Fault lines fracturing rock into particles underground and then those particles undergoing great heat and pressure

Question 29 refers to the following graph.

Rainfall in 5 Cities in California, 2008–2010

	2008–2009 Rain (in.)	2009–2010 Rain (in.)
Crescent City	49.35	62.77
Eureka	29.75	44.51
Ukiah	22.68	40.52
Redding	23.71	30.45
Sacramento	16.33	20.74

Source: Golden Gate Weather Services

29. Which city had the median increase in rainfall between the two time periods displayed in the table? Write your answer in the box below.

30. Brock's physics teacher has assigned everyone in his class the task of conducting an experiment. To write up their experiments, everyone must use the outline provided below.

Match each summary of the steps in Brock's experiment to the appropriate category in the experiment outline.

Experiment outline	Brock's steps
Step 1. Formulate a question about a phenomenon	
Step 2. Collect data	
Step 3. Form a hypothesis	
Step 4. Test the hypothesis through an experiment	
Step 5. Draw a conclusion	

a. Brock placed wooden cubes that were 1 cc, 10 cc, and 100 cc in water. He observed their buoyancy. Then he placed iron cubes of 1 cc, 10 cc, and 100 cc in water and observed their buoyancy.
b. Brock noted that ice floats in water, whether it is a small ice cube or a huge iceberg.
c. Brock said: "Since all wooden cubes float and all iron cubes sink, size does not affect the buoyancy of an object in water."
d. Brock asked, "Does size affect the buoyancy of an object in water?"
e. Brock thought: "For an object made of a given material, increasing the size of the object won't affect its buoyancy in water."

31. In 1993, after years of fluctuating water levels in their reservoir, the residents of Weyland County built a dam at one end of the reservoir to regulate and stabilize the water levels. Circle the X on the graph below that most likely represents 1993.

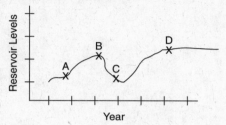

32. One property of a gas is that its molecules spread out to fill their container. Which of the following best illustrates this property of gases?

○ A. A teacher's perfume can be detected at the back of the classroom.
○ B. Rain puddles evaporate more quickly when the sun comes out.
○ C. Water is produced when hydrogen gas is burned in oxygen gas.
○ D. Liquid oxygen is denser than gaseous oxygen.

Directions Read the article and respond to the writing prompt below. Type your response on a computer, if one is available. If you do not have access to a computer, write your response neatly on paper. This task may require approximately 10 minutes to complete.

Plants grow faster when humans talk to them, but it is not clear why. Some scientists have hypothesized that it is the actual air involved that makes the difference. When we speak, we exhale carbon dioxide. Increased levels of carbon dioxide improve a plant's ability to grow, so this may explain why talking helps plants. Others have hypothesized that the benefit to plants comes from the content of what is being said. They hypothesize that it is the words themselves and their positive meaning that increase a plant's growing ability.

Write a Short Answer Response

Describe an experiment that could be used to test the two hypotheses described above.

Answers and explanations begin on page 119.

STOP

Congratulations! You have completed the GED® Science Practice Test.

Reminder: your next step is to check your answers with the
Practice Test Answers and Explanations and fill in the evaluation
charts that follow those explanations.

PRACTICE TEST ANSWERS AND EXPLANATIONS

Pages 105–117

1. **A. lift** As the diagram shows and the paragraph implies, the wing's weight and the opposing force of the air under it result in an upward force called *lift*.

2. **C. "Why We Sleep"** The topic of the paragraph is why sleep evolved in humans, and the paragraph cites several reasons for sleeping. The other options are too specific.

3. **17** If the mean is 23 degrees, then the sum of all six angle measurements must be $23 \times 6 = 138$ degrees. Since the five given angles add up to 121 degrees, the sixth angle must make up the difference, or $138 - 121 = 17$ degrees.

4. **B. the air and rainwater in the soil** According to the diagram, nitrogen-fixing bacteria take nitrogen from both the air and rain found in soil.

5. **C. The recycling of nitrogen through the biosphere involves many complex processes.** This is a general statement, or conclusion, that is supported by the various details in the diagram. The other statements are details from the diagram.

6. **B. compost with plant and animal wastes** According to the diagram, plant and animal waste contains nitrogen compounds that decomposers, including nitrite bacteria and nitrate bacteria, break down. In this way, composting with plant and animal wastes results in the addition of usable forms of nitrogen to the soil. So composting with organic waste (plant and animal materials) would be an alternative to synthetic fertilizers.

7. **D. For the three compounds shown, solubility increases as temperature increases.** The graph shows all three substances having increased solubility as the temperature rises from 0°C to 50°C. None of the other statements is supported by information in the graph.

8.

Step of the scientific method	The scientist's action
Step 1. Formulate a question about a phenomenon	b. The scientist wondered whether water at different temperatures might affect houseplants differently.
Step 2. Collect data	c. The scientist researched the growth rate of plants at various greenhouses, some of which use cool water and some of which use warm water to water their plants.
Step 3. Form a hypothesis	e. The scientist guessed that warm water might be better for plants than cool water.
Step 4. Test the hypothesis through an experiment	a. For 6 weeks, the scientist used water at 75 degrees to water plants in Group A and used water at 55 degrees to water plants in Group B. He recorded their growth during this period.
Step 5. Draw a conclusion	d. At the end of 6 weeks, the plants in Group A were, on average, 2" taller than plants in Group B. The scientist interpreted this to mean that warm water is better for plants than cool water.

9. **A. Its charge would become positive.** If an atom loses an electron, it has more protons than electrons, and thus it has a net positive charge. (Such an atom is called a positive ion.)

10. **A. the cracking of granite from the expansion of freezing water** This is an example of physical weathering because it involves changes of temperature causing physical effects on rock. Choice (C) is not an example of weathering because transport is involved.

11. **C. how special fluids keep insects alive during subfreezing weather** Understanding how insects can survive freezing may be a key to finding a way to freeze organs without destroying them.

12. **B. sea star** Of the four animals shown, only the sea star has a center section from which similar parts radiate. All the other animals are bilaterally symmetrical.

13. **C. Hydrogen peroxide is decomposing into water and oxygen.** The chemical reaction begins on the left hand side of the equation, which represents two hydrogen peroxide molecules. Thus, it is incorrect to say that hydrogen peroxide is being made (choices (A) or (D)). Rather, hydrogen peroxide is decomposing, or breaking up, into two substances. What remains after the chemical reaction is written on the right hand side of the equation. The question stem explains that water is composed of two hydrogen atoms and an oxygen atom, so the results of the reaction are water and O_2, which you can infer represents oxygen. Choice (B) is incomplete and (C) is correct.

14. **A. Mercury and bromine are liquids at room temperature.** Room temperature is about 70°F. The chart indicates that both mercury and bromine are liquids at that temperature: each has a melting point—the temperature at which it becomes a liquid—well below room temperature.

15. **D. Bacteria quickly evolved resistance to antibiotic drugs.** In 1969, the Surgeon General did not anticipate that bacteria would evolve to be resistant to the antibiotics that had been so effective until that time.

16. **B. The student should have used books of the same height for all of the ramps.** The height of the ramp affects how far the ball rolls. So the height of the ramp should be a controlled variable in this experiment. By using one ramp that is not as high as the others, the student is introducing a second variable into the experiment, which makes her data invalid for the ramp that is lower than the others.

17. **D. The dog has canines and the sheep does not.** If you compare the two diagrams, you will see that the sheep does not have any canines; instead the sheep has a large gap where the canines would be.

18. **C. The five largest asteroids are all farther from the sun than Earth is.** According to the chart, Earth's distance from the sun is set at 1, so any value greater than 1 indicates that the asteroid is farther from the sun than Earth is. All the asteroids have distance values of 2 or greater, so they are all farther from the sun than Earth is.

19. **less than** If all the lobsters weighed the maximum of 9 lbs, the 220 million pounds of lobster would still account for more than 20 million individual animals. Two blue lobsters out of 20 million lobsters is substantially less likely than the estimated 1 in 2 million occurrence of the blue mutation.

20. **A. Pressure builds up inside the magma chamber and vent.** If you examine the diagram, you will see that hot magma wells up into the volcano's cone. You need to infer that when the pressure builds up sufficiently, the volcano explodes, or erupts. None of the other events described would cause a violent explosion from the inside of the volcano.

21. **B. when food is digested, as when an enzyme in saliva called ptyalin breaks down starch into sugars without itself changing** The catalyst is the enzyme ptyalin; you can identify ptyalin as the catalyst, because it aids the chemical reaction of digestion but itself remains unchanged after the reaction. None of the other reactions include a substance that remains unchanged.

22. **B. People can reduce their chances of developing age-related hearing loss by not smoking.** Of all the options, this is the only one that is a hypothesis that the researchers could have been testing with their experiment. Choice (A) is too general to be a hypothesis for this experiment and is stated more like a conclusion than a hypothesis. The other options are facts relating to the study.

23. **D. Humans contain a higher percentage of carbon than bacteria do.** To find the correct answer, you must check each statement against the graphs to see whether the information in the graphs supports the statement. The graphs show that humans have a higher percentage of carbon than bacteria have.

24. **B. Both involve effort applied with circular motion.** The diagrams show that the effort applied to each of these machines is circular.

25. **A. During an ice age, temperatures drop and ice covers vast areas of Earth.** According to the passage, scientists aren't sure what causes ice ages. Choices (B), (C), and (D) each offer a different hypothesis for what causes an ice age. By contrast, choice (A) is an objective fact.

26. **D. The arrangement of the carbon, hydrogen, and oxygen atoms in the two hydrocarbons is different.** Although ether and ethanol both have the same number of carbon, hydrogen, and oxygen atoms, the different arrangements of atoms in each compound results in two substances with different properties.

27. **D. Observation is useful as long as the results are used to support or disprove a hypothesis.** According to Darwin's remarks, it is a waste of time to observe phenomena if you do not use what you observe to evaluate your theories.

28.

Type of process	Example of process
Magmatic	b. A gradual increase in temperature in the mantle, followed by a sudden drop in temperature
Hydrothermal	c. Movement of seawater through fractured rock underground
Metamorphic	d. Fault lines fracturing rock into particles underground, and then those particles undergoing great heat and pressure
Surficial	a. Wind eroding away the softer components in sandstone

29. **Crescent City** Begin by finding each increase in rainfall:

Crescent City	13.42
Eureka	14.76
Ukiah	17.84
Redding	6.74
Sacramento	4.41

The median is the middle value in a group of numbers. Arrange the numbers above in order; the middle value belongs to Crescent City.

30.

Experiment outline	Brock's steps
Step 1. Formulate a question about a phenomenon	d. Brock asked, "Does size affect the buoyancy of an object in water?"
Step 2. Collect data	b. Brock noted that ice floats in water, whether it is a small ice-cube or a huge iceberg.
Step 3. Form a hypothesis	e. Brock thought: "For an object made of a given material, increasing the size of the object won't affect its buoyancy in water."
Step 4. Test the hypothesis through an experiment	a. Brock placed wooden cubes that were 1 cc, 10 cc and 100 cc in water. He observed their buoyancy. Then he placed iron cubes of 1 cc, 10 cc and 100 cc in water and observed their buoyancy.
Step 5. Draw a conclusion	c. Brock said: "Since all wooden cubes float and all iron cubes sink, size does not affect the buoyancy of an object in water."

31.

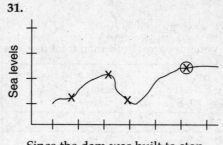

Since the dam was built to stop fluctuation, or change, in reservoir levels, 1993 must be the final year that reservoir levels changed.

32. A. A teacher's perfume can be detected at the back of the classroom. This is an example of diffusion, the spreading of gas molecules (perfume vapor) throughout a container (the classroom).

Short Answer: Experiment Design
Based on the following criteria, give yourself a score from 3 to 0 on your short written answer.

Score	Experiment Design	Data Collection Method	Criteria for Hypothesis Explanation
3	Complete	Well Formulated	Complete
2	Logical	Logical	Logical
1	Minimal	Minimal	Minimal
0	None	None	None

My Score: _____

PRACTICE TEST EVALUATION CHART

Questions 1–32

Circle the numbers of the questions that you got correct and then total them in the last column of each row.

	Life Science Pages 42–61	Earth and Space Science Pages 62–75	Physical Science Pages 76–91	Number Correct
Science Practices				
Comprehend Scientific Presentations Pages 26-27	2, 4, 17, 23	20	1, 24	____/7
Use the Scientific Method Pages 28–29	8, 11, 22	27, 28	16, 30	____/7
Reason with Scientific Information Pages 30–31	5, 15	18, 25	7, 9, 14	____/7
Express and Apply Scientific Information Pages 32–33	6, 12	10, 29	13, 21, 26, 32	____/8
Use Statistics and Probability Pages 34–35	19	31	3	____/3
SUBTOTAL	____/12	____/8	____/12	

Science Composite Score

Add your Subtotals as shown below to get the total number of points you earned on the *Science Test*.

Questions 1-32	_____/32
Explanation Short Answer	_____/ 3
Experiment Design Short Answer	_____/ 3
TOTAL	_____/40

If you do not have time to review the entire *Science* unit, you may want to review the sections that need the most work. You can use your total above (____/40) to figure out your percentage correct for the entire *Science* test. Divide the numerator by the denominator and multiply by 100.

GED® SCIENCE TEST RESOURCES

TI-30XS CALCULATOR REFERENCE SHEET

An on-screen calculator reference sheet, similar to what appears on these two pages, will be available to you on Test Day. However, you should understand how to use the calculator before you take the GED® Test.

To perform basic arithmetic, enter numbers and operation symbols using the standard order of operations.

Example: 8 × (−) 4 + 7 enter   −25

To calculate with percentages, enter the number, then 2nd (

Example: 4 0 2nd (× 5 6 0 enter   224

To perform calculations with scientific notation, use the ×10ⁿ key.

Example: 7 . 8 ×10ⁿ 8 ◄► − 1 . 5 ×10ⁿ 8 enter   630000000

To perform calculations with fractions, use the $\frac{n}{d}$ key. The answer will automatically be formatted in reduced form.

Example: $\frac{n}{d}$ 2 ▼ 9 ◄► × $\frac{n}{d}$ 3 ▼ 7 enter $\frac{2}{21}$

To perform calculations with mixed numbers, use 2nd $\frac{n}{d}$

As with fractions, the answer will automatically be formatted in reduced form.

Example: 1 2 2nd $\frac{n}{d}$ 5 ▼ 6 ◄► − 1 2nd $\frac{n}{d}$ 1 ▼ 2 enter $\frac{34}{3}$

To perform calculations with powers and roots, you will use the following keys:

| √/x^2 | $x\sqrt{}$ / ^ | 2nd | √/x^2 | 2nd | $x\sqrt{}$ / ^ |

Example: [1] [.] [2] [√/x^2] (enter)   **1.44**

Example: [7] [^] [4] (enter)   **2401**

Example: (2nd) [√/x^2] [5] [2] [9] (enter)   **23**

Example: [3] (2nd) [^] [1] [7] [2] [8] (enter)   **12**

The answer toggle key (◂▸) can be used to toggle the display result between fraction and decimal answers, exact square root and decimal, and exact pi and decimal.

Example: [$\frac{u\frac{n}{d}}{n}$] [9] (●) [1] [0] (enter) (◂▸)   **0.9**

Æ SYMBOL TOOL EXPLANATION

Starting in 2014, test-takers will take the GED® Test on the computer. On the computer-based test, some fill-in-the-blank questions require you to insert mathematical symbols.

You can access the "Symbol Selector" by clicking on this icon when it appears on the computer screen:

Æ Symbol

Choose the symbol you want, and click on Insert at the bottom of the screen. When you are done, close the screen.

Æ Symbol

∏	∫	≥	≤	≠	²	³	|	×	÷	±	∞	√
+	−	(	)	>	<	=

Below are the meanings of the symbols. Learn the meanings before you take the test because only the symbols will be available to you.

∏ "pi" symbol π

∫ "function" symbol

≥ greater than or equal to

≤ less than or equal to

≠ not equal to

² 2 exponent ("squared")

³ 3 exponent ("cubed")

| "absolute" value

× multiplication sign

÷ division sign

± "positive-or-negative" sign

∞ "infinity" symbol

√ "square root" symbol

+ plus sign or "positive" symbol

− minus sign or "negative" symbol

(open (or left) parenthesis

) close (or right) parenthesis

> "greater than" symbol

< "less than" symbol

= "equals" sign

INDEX

Endocrine system, 46
Endothermic reactions, 80
Energy
    activation energy, 80
    as natural resource, 64
    cell processes, 44
    conservation of, 82
    definition, 82
    ecosystems, 56
    endo- vs. exothermic reactions, 80
    forms of, 82
    heat, 70, 78, 80, 82
    mass relationship, 82
    momentum, 84
    nuclear reactions of stars, 70
    potential vs. kinetic, 82
    quasars, 70
Environment
    ecosystems, 56
    natural resources, 64
    population stress, 65
Enzymes, 46
Equations
    equals sign on toolbar, 125
Equator, 62, 66
Esophagus, 46
Eukaryotic cells, 42
Evaporation, 56, 78
Evidence. *See also* Evidence-based writing
    Science, 26, 30, 36
Evidence-based writing
    Short-Answer questions, 36
Evolution, 54
Exothermic reactions, 80
Experiments, 28, 36
Exponents
    Symbol Selector toolbar, 125
Extended Responses
    pretests, 1

F

Facts, 26
Fats as nutrients, 49
Faults in crust, 62
Fill-in-the-blank questions
    Mathematical Reasoning, xiii
    Science, 22
    Symbol Selector toolbar, xvi, 125
Flag for Review, 22, 50, 80
Food web, 56
Force

definition, 84
    electricity, 86
    in pairs, 84
    work and, 82
Formulas
    energy and mass, 82
Fossil fuels, 64
Fractions
    on calculator, 123, 124
Freezing points, 78
Friction as force, 84
Fronts (weather), 66
Functions (math), 125

G

Galápagos Islands, 54
Galaxies, 70
Gaseous state, 78
Generators, 86
Genetic material
    cell structure, 42
    chromosomes, 52
    genes, 50, 52
    genetic code, 52
    genetic engineering, 52
    human genome, 52
Geographic isolation, 54
Geothermal energy, 64
Germs, 48
Glucose, 44
Gold (Au), 76
Graphic information
    labels, 42
Gravity
    black holes, 70
    force, 84
    galaxies, 70
    solar system, 68
    weight and, 78
Greater than sign, 125
Guanine, 52

H

Habituation, 48
Heart, 46
Heat
    as energy, 82
    exothermic reactions, 80
    stars, 70
    states of matter, 78, 82

Poles of magnets, 86
Pollution, 64
Population
    natural resources, 64
Potential energy, 82
Power (energy), 82
Power (math)
    on calculator, 124
Precipitation, 56, 66
Predictions
    probability for, 34
    science reasoning, 30
Pretests
    next step after taking, 15, 118
    purpose, 15, 118
    Study Planners, 20
Probability
    independent vs. dependent, 34
    Science, 34
Producers (ecosystems), 56
Products of reaction, 80
Prokaryotes, 42
Prompt. *See* Writing prompt
Proportions, 80
Proteins, 48, 52
Protons, 76
Protostars, 70
Psychological dependence, 48
Pulsars, 70
Purebred traits, 50

Q

Quasars, 70
Questions. *See also* Extended Responses;
    Multiple-choice questions
    drag-and-drop, xv, 23
    drop-down, xiv, 22
    fill-in-the-blank, xiv, 22
    Flag for Review, 22, 50, 80
    hot-spot, xv, 22–23
    scientific method, 28
    Short-Answer, 23, 24, 36
    Symbol Selector toolbar, xvi, 125

R

Radiation from Big Bang, 70
Range of data, 34
Rate problems
    acceleration, 84
    speed, 84

Reactants, 80
Reaction from action, 84
Recessive alleles, 50
Rectum, 46
Recycling resources, 64
Red giant stars, 70
Reference sheet for calculator,
    123–124
Renewable resources, 64
Reproduction, asexual vs. sexual, 50
Reproductive system, 46, 52
Resources for GED. *See also* Natural resources
Respiration (cellular), 44
Respiratory system, 46
Revising and editing responses
    computer tools, 25
Ribonucleic acid (RNA), 52
Rocks in Earth structure, 63
Roots
    on calculator, 124
    symbol for, 125

S

Saliva, 46
Satellites, 66, 68
Saturn, 68
Science
    calculator for, 24, 34
    computer-based format, 22–25
    designing experiments, 36
    earth science, 62–75
    Flag for Review, 22, 50, 80
    highlighter tool, 25, 36
    life science, 42–61
    math problems on, 24
    physical science, 76–91
    science practices, 21, 26–41
    scientific method, 28, 36
    score needed to pass, 21
    Short-Answer questions, 23,
        24, 36
    space science, 62–75
    wipe-off board, 24, 36
Scientific notation, 123
Sea floor spread, 62
Semiconductors, 86
Sexual reproduction
    asexual versus, 50
    cloning, 52
    genetics, 52
    natural selection, 54

Venus, 68
Villi, 46
Viruses, 48
Vitamins as nutrients, 49
Volcano sources, 62
Voltage, 86
Volume
  states of matter, 78

W

Warm fronts, 66
Water (H_2O)
  cellular respiration, 44
  Earth's surface, 68
  ecosystems, 56
  formation equation, 79

natural resource, 64
nutrient, 48
photosynthesis, 44
rust, 80
states of matter, 78
universal solvent, 78
Watts, 82
Weather, 66
Weight, 78
White dwarfs, 70
Wind, 64, 66
Wipe-off board
  Mathematical Reasoning, xvi
  Science, 24, 36
Wire (electricity), 86
Work and energy, 82
Workers. *See* Labor